The Purposed, Healthy

and

Determined Leader

Justin Hammonds

Inspire Publications

A Division of

Inspire Consultants

For information about special discounts for bulk purchases, please contact
sales@inspireconsultants.com

Inspire Consultants can bring this author to your live event. For more information or to book an event contact
speakers@inspireconsultants.com

Cover Photo by Nathan Mantor Photography

Nathanmantorphotography.com

ISBN-10:0615465668

ISBN-13:978-0615465661

An army of sheep led by a lion
would defeat an army of lions led
by a sheep.

-Arab proverb

"Being busy does not always mean real work. The object of all work is production or accomplishment, and to either of these ends there must be forethought, system, planning, intelligence, and honest purpose, as well as perspiration. Seeming to do is not doing."

-Thomas A. Edison

This book is dedicated to:

My wife Kristie, your leadership and purpose have changed the lives of countless people. You are amazing! Thank you for sharing your life with me.

My three children, Morgan, Wyatt, and Colton, you have taught me more about life and love than I ever thought possible.

Tracy Plaisance: Thank you for all the leadership lessons.

The Hammonds and Messer Family.

Acknowledgments

Special thanks are in order to the following world renowned coaches and mentors: John Maxwell, Brian Tracy, Zig Ziglar and Brendon Burchard their work has inspired me to reach past my potential.

My Lord and Savior, Jesus Christ, I thank you for your grace and mercy. To you may the glory be.

Matthew 10:32

"Failure will never overtake me if my determination to succeed is strong enough."

Og Mandino

Table of Contents

Introduction 1

Chapter 1: *Self Development* 5

Chapter 2: *Purpose* 17

Chapter 3: *Healthy* 25

Chapter 4: *Determined* 35

Chapter 5: *Characteristics of a Great Leader* 43

Chapter 6: *Personality Types* 55

Chapter 7: *Influence* 65

Chapter 8: *Influence Endorsements and the Echo Effect* 75

Chapter 9: *Power Types* 81

Chapter 10: *Communication* 95

Chapter 11: *Motivation and Inspiration* 109

Chapter 12: *Vision and Developing Others* 123

Chapter 13: *P.H.D. Goal Reaching System* 139

Chapter 14: *Time Management* 147

Chapter 15: *The YOU Factor* 159

Chapter 16: *Putting It All Together* 179

Introduction

The principles contained within this book have been proven to be effective in the real world of leadership. I have been a student of leadership for over twenty years and have had the opportunity to lead and learn from some wonderful individuals. It is worth noting that I proudly profess that I am still and will forever be a student. I am on a journey to reach past my potential in all areas of my life and appreciate the chance to share some of the lessons that I have learned about life and leadership with you.

You'll notice that throughout this book I won't refer to becoming a good leader as the goal. Who strives to just be good at something? I want to strive to be GREAT! Who remembers good leaders? People remember GREAT Leaders. I have had the privilege of working alongside, and following, a full spectrum of leaders. Whether those leaders were good or bad, I have always looked for the leadership lessons to be learned. I have witnessed firsthand the growth and the demise of some of those leaders. I have had the opportunity to be mentored by some incredible people one of which is Tracy Plaisance.

Introduction

Becoming a great leader is about inspiring life-changing development in the people you touch. It's about helping them to reach past their potential and in the process, reaching past your own potential. The rewards for all involved with great leaders are many, but I suspect the greatest rewards are wrapped up in the relationship.

If you've had some of the same experiences that I have had within the spectrum of leaders, then you will agree that many of our "leaders" today seem to be lost. They seem to be accidental leaders. I'm convinced that we are suffering from the lack of leadership in every facet of society—schools, government, churches, civil organizations, and law enforcement, certainly it is present in the business world in which I operate. The evidence is overwhelming that we have grown a generation of accidental leaders. How did this happen? We live in the most exciting age known to man. We have so much information. You could find thousands of books written on leadership and for the most part, have them in your hands in minutes. Yet we settle for accidental leaders in every walk of our life. Often making excuses or giving them passes for their lackluster leadership. WHY? Perhaps we are just so busy. Maybe it's the age of information overload. Or maybe we have lowered our leadership expectations. Regardless of the cause the time for action is now! The time has come to start developing great leaders to fill the positions we value. I believe we are approaching a great revolution in leadership. I am convinced we have the tools necessary to develop and inspire a new generation of leaders. I'm honored that you have allowed me to share my thoughts on leadership and life with you.

I have chosen to use simple and universal illustrations rather than specific industry examples. I believe that these common illustrations serve a broader cross section and are easier to relate to your specific situations. You will not find fancy words and phrases in this book but what you will find is common words with an incredible meaning. The message is clear, and it has the power to change not only your leadership but also your life. Throughout this book *he* is used as a generic term to mean both male and female.

The road to becoming a great leader is a road filled with self-development and enlightenment. Truly great leaders are those who know themselves and are always challenging themselves to reach higher levels. I want to inspire you to start thinking in terms of reaching past your potential! And ultimately encourage you to develop others to reach past their potential as well!

Chapter 1:
Self Development

"Formal education will make you a living;
self-education will make you a fortune."

Jim Rohn

P.A.D. System for Learning

It's clear that the majority of us, throughout our formal education, have been taught to memorize information for testing purposes. Most have never been taught or exposed to a system for the practical application of knowledge gained. I found myself in this exact position. I realized that I had no real system for sorting the information I was learning much less applying the knowledge I was gaining. I must ask, what is the purpose of knowledge? I believe that the purpose of knowledge is to effect change, to move one to action, or use it in application. Surely it's not to acquire knowledge and never use or share it.

Years ago I developed a simple system for sorting information I call it P.A.D. This system has proven to be effective and reliable. If you like it, consider it yours; if you don't, develop a system that works for you.

I realized that I was missing a lot of opportunities to gain knowledge and information because I wasn't able to capture the idea and then properly categorize it. What I began to do was simple—I started to carry a pen and notebook or three-by-five cards. As I heard an interesting piece of information or a thought, I would write it down. I then would put it into one of three categorizes. As I became more of a student, I carried an electronic voice recorder in my vehicle. So as I listened to audio books or a lecture series, I could quickly capture my initial thoughts about what moved me. I cannot begin to describe how this has accelerated my thinking. When I opened my mind and put it on alert for information, it became like a strong magnet, just like radar looking for opportunities to learn. This simple technique has changed my life. The same is true when I was reading a book or studying material. I would underline and then categorize that particular topic or thought. This gave me an immediate reference point for the material; I would transfer that information into a notebook. I use this notebook for information and thoughts, and I go back to the notebook often to review what I have written. This notebook of my thoughts and information, distilled and continually refined, has been a valuable tool for me. It is like an open well available to quench the thirst for learning. I encourage you to do the same with the information you deem valuable; document your thoughts, expand and elaborate on the subject, and ultimately make it your own. This will result in tremendous growth and move you to action.

As I already mentioned, I put this information into categories by putting a P, A, or D next to the underlined topic or notes that I had taken.

The Three Categories

PROCESS: This means that you need to spend some more time thinking about this subject or idea to see if it applies to you and your situation. Many times you will come across information that is valuable but not necessarily practical for you.

ACTION: Any thought or idea that resonates with you that you can apply immediately or in the near future, should be placed in this category.

DEVELOP: Undoubtedly, you will be exposed to an idea that you will see value in but that needs to be developed for your situation and circumstance. This is where you classify this information. This is perhaps some of the most valuable information you will ever have. This information/knowledge will force you to really make it your own, and when you do this you have a greater chance of affecting change.

Consistently organizing information in a simple system will make you a better student and much better at applying the knowledge you gain. The more you apply the more effective and efficient you will become. There are those who become career collectors of knowledge but fail to apply this valuable asset. I urge you to be more than a collector—become an applier.

Why Do You Want to Be a Leader?

At the leadership seminars and workshops that I conduct, I'm often approached by individuals who are struggling in leadership roles. One of the first questions I ask is why do you want to be a leader? The way they answer the question reveals a lot about their motivation. The motivation tends to reveal the issues they might be facing. I have had some actually say that they don't want to be a leader, but they were promoted to a leadership role. Others have claimed that the "job" pays more. It's obvious that these individuals will always struggle because their motivation is not in line with what we know to be true about great leaders. Others have said they want to help develop and shape people and that they have goals and dreams they want to accomplish. These are the people who have the correct motivation. It's the desire to accomplish something more than you are capable of accomplishing alone. It's the desire to share that with others and help others reach past their potential. That is the motivation that will allow them to develop into great leaders.

Leadership carries a great deal of responsibility. There are no excuses for poor behavior as it pertains to leaders. Your followers will need to know that you are a person of character and part of that character is being responsible.

One of my favorite quotes from Zig Ziglar is "People don't care how much you know, till they know how much you care." This is true with leadership; do you think that those who are motivated by the pursuit of climbing a corporate ladder reflect the caring needed to attract high-level followers? It's impossible to disguise the motivation for your leadership for very long. Your followers will be able to detect those motives; your motives need to support your leadership mission. In order to reach high levels of leadership your desire and motivation must be more than to advance your career. So ask yourself what is my motivation for leadership? Is it all about me or is it about something much larger than myself?

You're a Leader to Someone

Regardless of if you know it or not chances are someone is looking to you for leadership at this very moment. Perhaps it is at work, church, civic events, or in your family, but the fact remains—you are a leader. Life works in such a way that we may never know who has given us the power of influence to lead them. One thing is certain: if they have given you the influence to lead, you have an obligation to become the greatest leader that you can be for them.

It's hard to imagine that there could be any more important leadership role than of being a leader for a child. Yet so many times this is the one we neglect the most. It's incredible to me to see how children respond to leadership. They possess some of the purest forms of followership you will ever experience. We have the potential of having the greatest impact on their life; we need to cherish this leadership role.

As you move through these thoughts on leadership, it's important that you keep your perspective on the wide scope of what leadership is while you consider the particular context in which you are leading. So many times we just want to apply our learned leadership at the workplace, but this is unwise. Leadership consumes every aspect of your life; leadership is about character, that is, who you are rather than whom you pretend to be. I submit to you that we would be better served by embracing our leadership role in every aspect of life and not just our professional world. The principles outlined here are universal and, to be effective, they must be applied to all aspects of your life.

Procrastination: The Frazier Law

The Frazier Law was developed while I was mentoring a dear friend of mine Jeff Frazier. Jeff by all accounts is the type of person you would like to have around—always volunteering for special projects and programs, he is just one of those fathers that inspire others and leave them wondering how he does it all. Jeff has a son with special needs and is also involved in the programs and functions of his two other children. In addition Jeff takes care of his ailing mother. Jeff had a real struggle with procrastination. However his procrastination was not about getting things done because he would. It was with life. It seemed like he could just never get focused on really living his life to the fullest. Sure, he was doing things, but those things were task orientated. His life had become a series of tasks that just began to run together. Throughout our many years of friendship, we would talk about this particular struggle of his. This type of procrastination can be difficult to detect, but it is common. Jeff was getting things done— more than most in fact. But he was merely surviving his life, just going through the motions. What Jeff and a lot of us do is medicate with tasks. We find ways to remove ourselves from the true reality of life by filling it full of tasks.

Jeff would often comment that he didn't have time to really put the energy into anything else because he was so busy. He was very busy using these tasks to hide from the reality of some serious issues within his life. Jeff was in a dead-end career, his personal relationships were less than fulfilling, and he had separated himself from fully living his life. Jeff used the tasks to distract himself from the reality that he had some life-changing events fast approaching, and he needed to make some major decisions that he, and only he, could make. The simple fact was, the more he could do to avoid this reality, the more comfortable he felt. So he loaded his schedule with more and more events and tasks. This is just like the person who medicates himself with alcohol or drugs to avoid or escape reality. Jeff was simply doing it with tasks. He didn't realize it and neither did I at first. But while he should have been actively and aggressively taking charge of his life, he was more and more consumed with tasks. They became excuses. He would often say that if he could just get his list down to a manageable size, then he would have some time to focus on these other areas. The Frazier Law can be summed up by stating:

For every one task that is accomplished, two more will be added to take its place.

Living your life by tasks is not living your life. We must realize that we have the power to decide where our life path takes us. As leaders, looking to lead and develop people, we must first believe that we have the power to develop ourselves. To develop the power within ourselves that gives us the ability to maximize our life and leave procrastination of any kind behind. This is not always a quick process but rather a life journey. Procrastinating will keep you from ever beginning this journey—thus robbing you from the happiness and joy that is yours to have.

Time is the most valuable resource we have. The clock is indiscriminate. It holds the same amount of time whether you are rich or poor. What makes successful people successful is what and how they decide to invest those hours. We need to make the shift from a mindset of spending time to a mindset of investing time. Those who live their life spending time seem to always be looking for more. However, successful people invest their time in high-value activities that produce freedom of time or time free from restrictions. The key is to objectively look at how you invest your time and make the changes that need to be made. As you move across the leadership continuum, it will be imperative that you have mastered this skill.

Both your personal and professional sides of life are susceptible to procrastination. Often procrastination begins in one area and quickly consumes the other. There are those, like Jeff, who can contain it in one aspect of their life. However, one aspect is one too many. I am happy to say that today Jeff has taken charge of his life and has made successful transitions and is living a P.H.D. life.

Successful people don't procrastinate. Great leaders are always successful. It would be nearly impossible to become a great leader and not be successful. Largely because of the self-development that becoming a great leader requires, it guarantees that you will be successful, regardless of how you measure success. Don't put off your success by procrastinating— embrace your success. Embrace the development process and enjoy the journey to greatness.

> "If I have the belief that I can do it, I will surely acquire the capacity to do it, even if I may not have it at the beginning."
>
> -Mahatma Gandhi

Reaching Past Your Potential

Perhaps the biggest travesty to one's self and society as a whole is living in a way so as to not reach your potential. Too many times in life we sell ourselves short and fail to realize the tremendous gift we have been given and the responsibility that we have to fulfill it. Most people are capable of far more than they think, but their complacency for mediocrity grows stronger every day.

We should reach past our potential! It is time that we stop selling ourselves short of what we can be. Our potential is not static, it is either growing or it is shrinking based on the activities and thoughts in which we participate. We need to be engaged in activities that keep our potential growing and our minds creating the endless possibilities for that potential.

I was taught a valuable lesson from Eric Enck whose company Enck Consulting has been providing valuable education and practical self-defense skills for women and children for years. Eric has been my personal self-defense instructor for the past decade. I first came to know him when he came to work for the police department with which I served. He soon made a huge impact in our organization and fast became one of the core team members. Eric is a fifth-degree black belt in Wado Ryu Karate and holds numerous belts in other martial arts disciplines. One day while we were working on punches and kicks, he said something to me that that has served as a valuable lesson. He was holding a bag that I was hitting, and he looked at me and said, "You're trying to punch the bag." I must admit that I had no idea what he was trying to convey to me, and he must have figured that out by the look on my face. He said, "You need to punch through the bag. You are limiting your power because you're only trying to punch the bag. The power comes not from hitting the target, but from punching through the target, driving completely through it." I'm sure a light bulb appeared over my head at that moment. This has become a metaphor I have used in every aspect of my life from that day forward. So often we just look at the target and think if we touch it, then we have succeeded. When the reality is the power comes not from the touch, but the drive of going through it. We shouldn't focus on just reaching our potential—we need to focus on reaching past our potential.

Chapter 2:
Purpose

"I am here for a purpose and that purpose is to grow into a mountain, not to shrink to a grain of sand. Henceforth I will apply ALL my efforts to become the highest mountain of all, and I will strain my potential until it cries for mercy."

Og Mandino

P.H.D. Success Formula

The P.H.D. Success Formula is a passion of mine. I developed this formula out of necessity. I was at a personal low point in my life. I doubted a career decision that I had made that removed me far from my comfort zone. Personally, I was struggling with my identity, and it was affecting every facet of my life in a negative way. I later learned that the things that I had identified as being problematic in my life were merely just the tip of the iceberg visible above the water; the larger issues that I had been avoiding were hidden below the water. I chose to deal with the whole iceberg and not just the portion that I could see. Truthfully, I had known there was more below the surface for years but had been avoiding it, content to sail around it. When my world began to crumble around me, I realized that I was going to have to deal with it all, and I became determined to melt it away. This is how the P.H.D. Success Formula began.

The formula is simple, it's easy to understand, and it's highly effective. The P is for purpose. The H is for healthy. The D is for determination. We can be successful in many areas of our lives and still not be truly successful. This is a concept that is hard for many of us to understand. As we walk through this, I believe that you will have a clearer picture of what true success might look like in your life. The first element in the philosophy is purpose.

The P: Purpose

On the surface it sounds so simple; we all know what purpose is. Take a closer and perhaps deeper look at what purpose is and what it can do to transform your life. Let's start by establishing the definition. Purpose is defined as "the reason for which something exists or is done, made, used; an intended or desired result; end; aim; goal; determination; resoluteness."(1)

Purpose. Do you have it in your life? In your business? In your organization? If so, what is it? If not, why not? We all have encountered people who live their whole life without purpose. Truly, their only purpose in life is to survive to the next day. I suppose in an extreme circumstance that is a viable purpose, but clearly that is not the case with most of us. I watch as so many people walk around aimlessly, just going through the motions day after day, month after month, year after year with little success and few results. Is this surprising? Not at all. People who live this way tend to just let life happen to them. As a result they become very good at creating excuses for why things fail to materialize. Often times they believe there is a conspiracy against their success. It is crucial that we understand how vital purpose is to our life. Purpose is a fundamental that cannot be overlooked.

With Purpose Comes Power

With purpose comes power. The most amazing thing happens when people or organizations have purpose. They become empowered. They become focused. They become driven. They begin to believe. They begin to move with determination. We must understand the power that comes from purpose before we can become great leaders.

When you become a person of purpose, you become a seeker of opportunities that ultimately lead to greater success. When you empower yourself with purpose, you begin to program your mind to recognize and seek opportunities to fulfill your purpose. Have you ever noticed that when you set your mind on wanting a particular item you suddenly begin to notice it more often? It could be a car, motorcycle, boat, house, clothes, computer, phone you name it. It doesn't matter; you will rapidly begin to see it everywhere. Before you came to the point of wanting it you may or may not have even noticed the item. Now suddenly it is everywhere. It happened when your desire became strong enough to make the decision that you wanted it. You programmed your subconscious mind to look for it, and to actively seek the opportunity to get it. If it's a car you might then decide on a specific feature

> People without purpose have less joy and fulfillment when compared to those who live life with purpose.

or customizations, your subconscious mind will begin to search for it in those specific details. This relates to anything that you have a strong desire for. We have all experienced it, and the incredible thing is your mind did this for you with no conscience effort on your part. You made a decision and it went to work for you. This is a powerful tool successful people and great leaders use. As powerful as this is, there are additional proven techniques you can use to help increase this natural phenomenon. I will outline those in Chapter 13 the Goal Reaching section.

Some of the most exciting moments in your leadership development will occur when you see purpose develop and grow in the individuals you lead. When their words and actions become focused and passionate about their purpose, it will only serve to increase yours. These are the types of people you need to surround yourself with to accelerate the reaching of your goals.

People without purpose have less joy and fulfillment when compared with those who live life with purpose. At times they rely on others to give them a purpose. This is impossible. Others cannot give you purpose. You must want your purpose and you must develop that purpose within yourself. Others can give you a reason, but they cannot give you purpose. It is true that others can help you find your purpose and even assist you in developing it, but they cannot give it to you.

There is a difference between reason and purpose. Often people mistakenly believe the two words have the same meaning. Reason is defined as "the basis or cause, as for some belief, action, fact, event."[2] As you can see there is a difference. Purpose is more involved. Purpose has a deeper commitment, purpose is the *why you exist*. Reason is the *what you have to do to exist*.

 Are you living with reason or purpose? You may be living with reason today, but as you start to live with purpose your life changes dramatically. How do you want to live your life, with reason or purpose?

How Do You Get Purpose?

Because of low self-worth we often repress what we already know about our purpose. Many times people are fearful of their purpose.

However, the first step of the purpose journey begins with the discovery and acceptance of your purpose. Once this occurs you, will find that the fulfillment begins to have a life of its own. The place you need to look for your purpose is within yourself. In Luke 12:34 of the Bible it says, "For where your treasure is, there your heart will be also." So when using the word purpose, we must think of the word heart. In regards to the treasure portion of that passage let me make this very clear, by NO means am I saying that when you find your purpose, that is where you'll find a fortune in money. I believe treasure can mean a lot of things, most of which are more valuable than money. Treasure will make you wealthy, however money is a small portion of wealth.

Listening to your heart is something most of us have never been taught. We have been conditioned to use our mind. When we live with reason that is exactly what we are doing. When we live with purpose we are using our heart. Unfortunately most of the world lives with reason and not purpose.

Here are some action exercises to start the process of listening to your heart.

• ***Invest time with yourself***

According to the A.C. Nielsen Company, the average American watches twenty-eight hours of television per week.(3) That is two months of nonstop TV watching per year. That's startling to me. The majority of this time is absolutely wasted. Take some time and invest it with yourself. Limit the outside stimulus that can distract your attention. The idea is for your thoughts to provide the stimulus.

- ### *Time in thought*

This goes hand in hand with investing time with yourself. The idea is to have a conversation with yourself, about yourself, all by yourself. Take a drive, a walk, a bike ride, or just sit in a quiet place—the point is to give yourself time to think. You may find your mind wandering, that's normal, just stick with it. Taking time to think about yourself and your future is always a wise investment.

- ### *Examine your core interests*

If you weren't concerned about money, what would you do? Where would you go? How would you allot your time? This is perhaps the best place to start to look for your purpose. Really explore this area; you might be surprised at what you discover.

These exercises are designed to get the process stared. Anything that is positive and can move you closer to yourself is recommended. The idea is to get to the heart of matter.

Sharing Your Purpose

Have you ever noticed that people with purpose seem to also have passion? They seem to enjoy every minute of what they are experiencing. It's contagious. Purposed people are passionate people. When you find your purpose you need to share it with others. As we mentioned, your purpose may be more than you can accomplish by yourself. Don't let this scare you. That means you need others, and those others need you. They will potentially become people who you will lead. Be aware that when you share your purpose with people that are living in a world driven by reason, they may not be able to appreciate your purpose. Don't let them deter you. There have been very few who have accomplished great things that didn't have their share of doubters.

Purpose: do you have it in your life? In your business? In your organization? If not, why not? If you do, what is it? Have you shared your purpose with the people who should know?

Chapter 3:
Healthy

"A healthy attitude is contagious but don't wait to catch it from others. Be a carrier."

Tom Stoppard

The H: HEALTHY

Healthy means more than the physical; it also encompasses mental, emotional, and spiritual aspects of your life. It is the balance between your personal and business life. As leaders, we often have difficulty separating the two. As a result our marriages, our children, and other relationships suffer and eventually fail. We must be healthy and balanced in all aspects of our lives. Without balance, the formula loses a significant portion of its power. The true power comes from purpose, health, and determination converging in your life to create a synergetic effect that accelerates your progress toward your goals.

A lot of people struggle with low self-worth. Notice I used the term self-worth not self-esteem. While some may argue the contrary, they are very different. Self-esteem has more to do with your perception of how others view you. Self-worth is how you view yourself. A healthy self-worth is more valuable than gold and will take you farther than any mode of transportation.

Low self-worth is an issue that affects all classes of life. You begin to develop self-worth at a very early age. Some experts say from childbirth the process of developing self-worth begins. At this stage of development your mind is like a new computer ready to receive and file information in all forms. The thoughts and feelings you have, as well as your surroundings, all have a tremendous impact on you. The way we were parented has lasting effects on self-worth. There are pivotal points in our life that shaped the way we view ourselves today.

As we grow our interaction and experiences continue to mold our self-worth.

You must develop the feeling and thoughts that you deserve to be successful. You must know you were not created to just be okay or to barely get by. You were created to be successful. You were created to be great and to accomplish great things. You have the potential to make a difference in the lives of many. As long as you believe your destiny is success, and you commit to the work necessary to fulfill that destiny, you will make a difference. Sure there will be points when you will struggle, most of us do. However, it is in the struggles that we become great.

If I told you that you couldn't fail and that you could have all you ever dreamed of. Would you believe me? I have come to the conclusion that it is true. In fact, these are guarantees. If your work is in proportion to your dreams and goals, success will be yours.

> You will continue to push away success until you establish a view that you deserve to be successful.

The only way to fail is to stop reaching for your goals and dreams. So often, we put time lines and constraints in areas of our life that we shouldn't and fail to put them in areas that we should. The first step toward success begins with your thoughts. When you embrace the thought and believe that you deserve an incredible life filled with all the things you desire, life looks and feels different.

Self-Worth Voice

We all have a self-worth voice, and it can be dramatically different from person to person. This is the voice years of experiences has created. It's the dialog for your inner thoughts and beliefs. If your voice is limiting, I want you to change it. Get rid of the dialog that limits you from reaching past your potential. Crush the voice that tells you "you can't" and lift up the voice that screams to you that "YOU CAN"! Like a child waiting for permission, your positive voice is waiting for your embrace. Empower your voice; unleash the voice with positive expectations that will speak to you about your unlimited opportunities. You can achieve, and you will be successful. The voice that has been holding you back for years has now become your biggest fan. The voice that has chained you to fear will now set you free with confidence. The voice that has told you to look for excuses is now seeking opportunities. This is your new powerful voice; this is your new best friend.

> "Never say anything about yourself you do not want to come true."
>
> -Brian Tracy

Ten Steps to Developing a Positive Self-Worth Voice

Here are ten steps you can implement today to develop and increase your positive self-worth voice. The more you work on developing this voice the stronger and louder it will become.

1.   *Realize that you are unique*

You were created as a unique being. Not to be a clone of someone else. We all possess unique qualities and gifts. You have strengths and talents that are unique to you. You must realize your uniqueness and embrace it. Explore it. Brand it. You own it! Whether anyone else understands it, you do, and you are the one that matters.

2.   *Accept compliments as sincere*

When our self-worth voice is not healthy we tend to believe others are not sincere and they are joking when paying us compliments. Stop! Trust that people are sincere and simply accept the compliment with a "Thank you." Don't make excuses for why they shouldn't compliment you, you're worthy of the compliment.

3.   *Use positive affirmations*

This is a tool that has been widely taught over the years. We have all heard the saying: You are what you believe. I believe that you are a person of value. You need to believe that too. By creating positive affirmations for all aspects of your life, you will start the day feeding your mind the positive food it craves.

 Here are some examples of affirmations.

• I am happy, focused, and seek opportunities.

• I am unique and I celebrate my uniqueness.

• All my relationships are positive and healthy.

- I love myself and treat myself with respect.

- I am valuable.

- I am confident and competent.

- I am successful and generous.

4. *Create a personal empowering statement*

Your personal self-worth voice will latch onto this statement and will begin to program your thinking to match it. This statement should be part of your daily affirmations. In the beginning you will have to read it. But soon when it is committed to memory you will be able to recite it with passion and conviction, you will find it becoming more and more empowering. The magic behind this is the more you commit yourself to the process, the more power it possesses. When you reach the point that you begin to share this with others, you will discover a self-worth voice so loud people and opportunities cannot help but listen.

5. *Establish a goal-reaching program*

Goals are like maps. They show us where we are going and how we will get there. Without these goals you are much like a ship drifting where the current takes it. That means you may never make landfall, or if you're fortunate enough to reach land, it might not be the place you wanted to be.

6. *Start a personal positive library*

This library should consist of books, audio books, seminars, video, magazines, and most importantly your notes and files. The catch to all of this is you must read, listen, or watch what is in your library. When you make this a priority your subconscious will go to work seeking out this type of information.

7. *Purge negative people and thoughts from your life*

This can be a difficult situation for us all. You must understand negative people are a weight around your neck. Every day they throw you into the metaphoric water. This is a tiring routine and will limit your progress. Negative people are like a disease to positive people. It takes a tremendous amount of effort and energy to stay positive and focused. Joe Murphy, one of my clients, often says, "If you hang around nine broke people, you soon will be the tenth." It's the same with negative people, but it doesn't take nine of them—one is enough to do considerable damage and derail your progress. There might be certain family dynamics that come into play that force you to have interaction with negative people. You must limit your time with this type of person and detox with positive activities. At the very least, you should never spend more time with negative people than you do with positive people and positive things.

8. *Write your story*

You don't have to become an author. You do need to write chapter titles and perhaps subchapters from the beginning to the present. You'll begin to see what have been pivotal points in your life. When you get to the present, really think about this. You are writing the story of your future, of how your life will be. Think of the incredible opportunity for you to live what you write. Will it be more of the same? Or will you reach past your potential and have the life you deserve and desire? The fact is you really are the author of your life. You really do have the power to change what you don't like and increase the things you do. Spend some time with this, and it will provide you with an incredible sense of empowerment. If you find yourself doubting your capabilities as you create your future, stop. Think about all you want and desire, and ask why not?

9.   ***Stop self-destructive behavior***

You have heard the saying "I'm my own worst enemy." The sad thing is it's more than likely true. We've become wrapped up in behaviors in which we should never have become involved in. We must stop this self-destructive behavior. Here are some of the areas that we often struggle with.

- Determining your self-worth by comparing yourself to others

- Confronting your fears

- Confronting your past

- Negative self-talk

- Trying to live to Hollywood standards

Negative reinforcement never produces positive results. We cannot be held hostage by our past or our fears. I find more often than not the reason we participate in self-destructive behavior is we don't feel like we deserve the best in life. Again this comes to play with the low self-worth that is raging like an epidemic in our society.

The past is behind you unless you choose to keep it in front of you. So many times we decide to walk backward in life, so we can keep our eye on the thing that caused us pain. While others are walking forward in life, we try to compare ourselves with them. It is very difficult to walk backward, and it's impossible to look both in front and behind at the same time. Yet many of us try. This breeds the thought that we are "falling behind," and this in turn increases those negative thoughts we tell ourselves. The only way to change this is to confront the issue that keeps you walking backward. Confront it, resolve it, dissolve it, and start walking facing forward. We are designed to move forward. It's with forward motion that we excel. So stop, confront it, resolve it, dissolve it, and start looking forward at your future.

10. *Engage in healthy activities*

Healthy activities include anything that is a positive. The only parameters are that the activity needs to be healthy for you. There is something that happens when you become active; activity produces the positive environment that one needs to develop properly.

I recently had the privilege to attend an event where the former First Lady, Laura Bush, spoke. During her talk she said that when George W. Bush took office as the forty-third president of the United States of America, she was repeatedly asked by the media what type of first lady she was going to be. Would she be more like Barbara Bush or Hillary Clinton? I found it refreshing when she said that "she had made up her mind that she was going to be Laura Bush." Even at the highest levels of society others are attempting to have you conform to a package that they see fit. We need to celebrate our uniqueness and individuality. Being you is the first step to greatness.

Chapter 4:
Determined

"It's hard to beat a person who never gives up."

Babe Ruth

The D: Determination

Y ou have the power and opportunity to change your life in dramatic ways. We live in a time where truly anything is possible. The newspapers, magazines, radio, TV, and the Internet are filled with people who believed in themselves and changed their lives. Recently, I was reading in Bloomberg Businessweek about a man who had purchased the Silverdome for less than $600,000. Located in the city of Pontiac, Michigan the Silverdome has 80,000 seats and was the location of the 1982 Super Bowl between the San Francisco 49ers and Cincinnati Bengals. The title caught my interest, but about halfway through the article, I became intrigued by the story of the man that had purchased it. The article outlines that Mr. Apostolopouslos migrated to Canada from Greece when he was just a teenager with very little English, $50.00, and a suitcase. He cut chicken behind a Kentucky Fried Chicken in Toronto and then began a janitorial business. His success with the janitorial business led to bigger opportunities and eventually real estate dealings. Today his wealth is estimated at 800 million dollars.[1] Clearly he is a self-made man.

When you take responsibility for your life and cease to make excuses, you will start the process of empowerment. Empowerment comes from you. You have it. You must believe in yourself and your abilities.

We were all born with a tremendous gift. It is the gift of determination. It's only through our experiences that we have been taught not to act on this determination. In the previous section on self-worth, I shared my belief that we allow our past experience to shape us today and that pivotal points in our life have set a tone and direction that we follow. It's the same with determination—our past experiences have either helped grow our determination or they have served to destroy it.

How does a baby learn to walk? Through its own determination to move. The baby, with determination, first learns to roll over. Then how to lift his head and move to his knees and slowly begins to crawl. The baby gets very good at crawling. Then one day he pulls himself up while holding onto something firm and falls. Over and over he pulls himself up. He holds on to a solid object, and then he lets go of the only thing that keeps him standing because it's also the thing that prevents him from walking. He takes his first wobbly step, and he falls. He is not discouraged—he is determined. So he tries again and again and only after countless times does he learn the art of balance. Then soon that determination to walk turns into the determination to run. It all started with the determination to move. Not one of us would prevent a baby from learning to walk regardless of how long it took. The baby knows that it must learn to move, and it must learn to walk regardless of how impossible it must seem. Without the gift of determination from birth the baby would never be able to overcome such a great obstacle. Yet we discount the gift of determination with which we have been born, settling for the thoughts and fear that has been taught to us.

> "Opportunity often comes disguised in the form of misfortune, or temporary defeat."
>
> -Napoleon Hill

You might be at the point in your life that you desperately need to change. Like the baby learning to walk, you are facing obstacles that seem too large. Realize you have a spirit of determination; know you are a determined individual. Hold onto a firm object and begin to start to take the steps necessary to move in the direction you need to go. You can change your life. You are a determined person. You will achieve, and you will be successful!

If you struggle with determination, you may be letting fear keep you from reaching past your potential. Work on your self-worth voice and look deep into your past experiences to see how they have imprisoned your determination. Remember this powerful formula for gaining control over your past experiences: Confront it, resolve it, dissolve it, and move forward."

Fear of Failure

Fear of failure is the enemy of determination. From an early age we have been taught the wrong lessons about failure. We have been told failure will make you a loser. That failing is negative, and failing makes you wrong. We have been taught failure is the opposite of success, and if you are to become successful, you must avoid failure. If we were to put failure and success on a scale, they would be on the opposite ends.

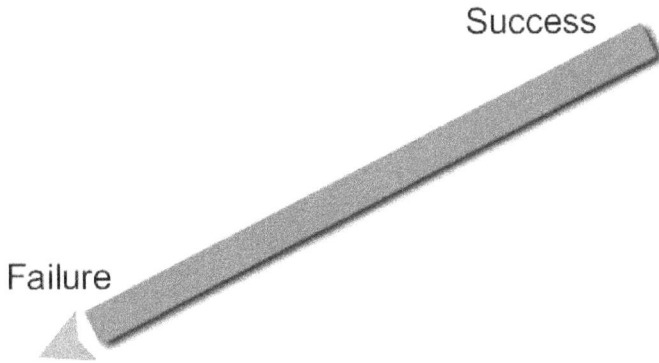

(Diagram 4.1)

What successful people have learned about failure is completely the opposite of what society is teaching. The reality is that failure is the prerequisite for success. It is a string of failures that pave the way for success. They are not on the opposite end of the spectrum—they are side by side. There is no way around it; it is truly what makes the success so meaningful.

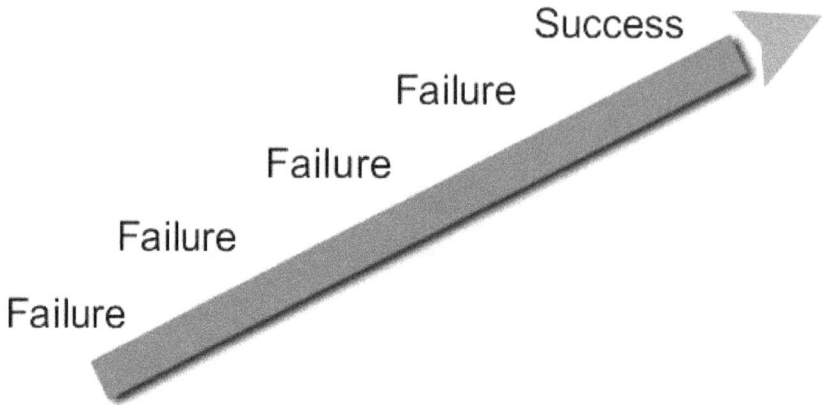

Success

Failure

Failure

Failure

Failure

(Diagram 4.2)

If you were to study any of the great successes in history, you would clearly see that through the failure is what made the success. It was the many attempts that led to success we recognize and enjoy about them. Let me share with you a string of quotes by one of the greatest inventors America has ever produced, Thomas Edison.

"I have not failed. I've just found ten thousand ways that won't work."

"I am not discouraged, because every wrong attempt discarded is another step forward."

"Nearly every man who develops an idea works at it up to the point where it looks impossible, and then gets discouraged. That's not the place to become discouraged."

"Many of life's failures are men who did not realize how close they were to success when they gave up."

Michael Jordan is considered by many to be the greatest basketball player to ever play the game. A player that at any time had tens of thousands of eyes watching his every move on the court, and yet he speaks of failure this way, "I've missed more than nine thousand shots in my career. I've lost almost three hundred games. Twenty-six times I've been trusted to take the game winning shot and missed. I've failed over and over and over in my life. And that's why I succeed!"

We must stop associating negative thoughts and feelings with failure. We need to celebrate the attempt. We need to recognize it is the pursuit of accomplishment, the pursuit of reaching past our potential that makes great success. It is not, nor has it been or ever will be, those who are imprisoned with the fear of failure who will become successful. It is only those who embrace the truth about failure. The truth is failure moves you closer to success; failure is the roadmap to success. Small-minded people love to point a cynical finger at those who display the courage to fail. However the big thinkers know failure is part of the ingredients for success. Don't let this learned negative-thought pattern destroy your gift of determination.

Renewable Source of Energy

The challenge for this generation is finding a renewable source of energy. There is great debate about this, but regardless of what side you are on, we all agree it's necessary. I want to introduce to you the idea that the P.H.D. formula is just that for our lives. Think about your purpose as being the sun, and the importance it plays in the world. We know that the sun is the greatest energy known to man. It costs you nothing, and you don't even have to think about it, but it's there for you without fail. The sun is versatile, and it can be used to accomplish amazing things. But the sun is healthy because the moon balances it. Just as the moon becomes the most visible object in the sky at night, so should there be times for other priorities of the healthy person. The moon is vital for a healthy earth. The interesting thing is that the moon shines because of the sun. The sun, our purpose, is still there and continues to light the way. It's good, and it's necessary to have time without the direct sun. Just as the sun sets in the evening, it is determined to rise in the morning. It's determined to give us the light that we need to sustain life. It's determined to produce the light necessary to grow all the wonderful things that we enjoy. Just as the earth relies on the sun and the moon working together, we need the power of P.H.D. working in our lives to thrive.

Chapter 5:
Characteristics of a Great Leader

"Leadership is a combination of strategy and character.
If you must be without one, be without the strategy."

Gen. H. Norman Schwarzkopf

Manager vs. Leader

O ne of my first jobs when I was in high school was working at a health club in southern California, where I grew up. I worked there throughout high school and really enjoyed the job. By virtue of seniority, I was sometimes deemed the manager for the day. I remember feeling such a sense of pride that I was "in charge." I knew this was the beginning of a career in management. I continued to work that job basking in the moments of responsibility. Thus began my love affair with leadership.

I worked for two years in the California political scene. I was nineteen at the time and had a fluctuating staff of thirty-five to fifty. I was responsible for every aspect of the campaign—the hiring, firing, payroll, and daily operations. I really wasn't qualified for the job, but I had known Jerry from the health club, and I believe he liked me enough to give me an opportunity. Once hired, I rarely saw Jerry even though he was my direct supervisor; he trusted me and took a hands-off approach. As long as I was producing the desired results, Jerry gave me the space to learn. It was there I began to see the awesome responsibility of leadership. Even though at the time I couldn't understand it or appreciate the amazing opportunity I had been given. Looking back now twenty years later, I am thankful for the experience, and I am still learning lessons from that time period. It was there I began to see the difference between managing and leading.

A manager is described as a person who directs and controls resources, expenditures, and oversees tasks. While a leader is defined as a person who leads or guides, inspires, and has influence. There is a big difference between the two. While both are nouns, only one mentions the word influence. Influence is the key on which all leadership is predicated. We are all familiar with the word influence, but I find that few really know the meaning of it and even fewer understand the power of influence. Influence is the power affecting a person, thing, or course of events.

So putting this together from practical use, a manager is one who oversees tasks and directs projects. Managers have a level of control but not necessarily any meaningful influence. A leader is someone who guides and is in charge but also has influence. Influence is the ability to affect people. There are those who have the positions and titles of leaders, but are they really leading or are they managing? Do you have influence or just control? Perhaps you're unsure. If that's the case look at what is happening around you and examine the way your team operates. What type of influence do you have with them? The answers to these questions can be found in those you are leading.

Managers play an important role in any organization. They bring an incredible amount of value; I don't want you to think that they don't. Part of becoming a great leader is being able to identify great managers. However, we must be aware that there is a difference between managing and leading. We must embrace the fact that mangers that manage cannot substitute for leaders that lead.

So often we make the mistake of believing managers should be able to lead without ever giving them the benefit of development. It is imperative we prepare our team for success. We prepare them by developing them into leaders. It goes without saying you cannot develop others if you yourself are not developing. A fundamental part of becoming a great leader is self-development. The more you develop yourself and the others around you the more influence you will create. There are things you just can't measure on a spreadsheet, influence and development are two of those things.

It's imperative to understand being assigned a leadership position in an organization doesn't make you a leader, but it does make you a manager of the organization's assets. Leading is about people first and assets second. The most important asset a leader will ever have cannot be purchased; it is the gift of influence through followership. Obvious as it may seem, you cannot be a leader without having someone willing to follow you. Having a leadership title can help you create initial influence, however, it will not be sustainable without taking further steps to develop a deeper level of influence. This is one of the hardest lessons for new leaders to learn. As we grow and develop our leadership skills, we discover often times a title gets in the way of real leadership. We must remember the ability to influence is the key.

Characteristics of a Great Leader

Throughout many years of research and countless speaking engagements, I have had the privilege to share the principles outlined in this book. I have come to realize what makes a great leader really is universal. Regardless of age, sex, race, and religion, for the most part they are the same. If you were to write down the top ten things that makes a great leader what would they be? If you're like the majority of the people I have met, then your list will include some of these:

- Integrity

- Has purpose

- Honesty

- Good listener

- Dedication

- Vision

- Willingness

- Great communicator

- Positive attitude

- Energetic

- Passionate

- Motivated

- Open-minded

- Friendly/approachable

- Appreciative/grateful

- Gives credit and recognition

- Strives for greatness/excellence

- Does not accept failure

- Supportive

- Compassionate

- Places the team before self

- Knows their industry

- Not afraid to help out

- Trustworthy

- Not afraid to make decisions

Certainly the list doesn't stop here, but if you think about the qualities that you listed, you will notice very few have anything to do with job-specific attributes. Instead, they are mostly personal character traits. I find this true wherever I go. Truly GREAT leaders are those who have the core character traits that are listed above. Of course, you need to understand the industry that you are in, but you don't need to be an expert in every position of the organization to become a great leader. It's more about people, and less about job function. No matter where you are in your leadership walk, you must know that people, not things, are your business. If you are a leader, you are in the people business. It doesn't matter what industry in which you operate in, your business is people. It's about having a vision and getting people to believe in that vision. It's so much more than moving or selling one widget from here to there. Leaders have to know how to get others to buy-in to the vision and become purposed about that vision. We must learn the steps to having others give us the gift of influence.

Integrity is generally the first thing people list when it comes to great leadership. Why is that? It's because integrity is what matters most. The definition of integrity is "the adherence to moral and ethical principles; soundness of moral character; honesty."[1] It is impossible to become a great leader without integrity. Integrity is the foundation of leadership. Leaders have risen and leaders have fallen on this one principle. I can think of no other single more important element in leadership than integrity. The word integrity comes from the Latin word integer, which means to be "whole, complete, untainted, upright."[2] Looking at the character list you will notice that without integrity most of the others would not matter. There is a Chinese proverb that says, To starve to death is a small thing, but to lose one's integrity is a great one. An integrity violation is a stain that never goes away.

> Integrity is a choice, you choose to live and conduct your life with it or without it.

There are many great practical definitions of integrity the one I like the most is doing the right thing when no one else is around, and no one else will ever know. The responsibility of integrity is yours. No one else can have your integrity, and no one else can take your integrity away. There are no excuses. It's not good enough to live 95 percent of your life with it; it must be 100 percent of the time. Integrity is just that important!

As you embrace the P.H.D. philosophy you naturally will develop many of these core character traits such as being purposed, having a positive attitude, being passionate and motivated, having vision and energy, and wanting to strive for greatness. Certainly there are many more of these traits that will surface and become apparent to those you lead. As leaders, we need to make sure we aren't asking anything of our followers we wouldn't or haven't done ourselves. This one issue can drive a wedge between the leader and follower causing the leader to lose influence. In that same vein, the willingness to pitch in and get your hands dirty is always listed as a trait of a great leader. By doing just that you can affect a huge change in momentum. It can generate excitement and can have a positive ripple effect like a stone tossed into a pond. The lack of approaching situations with an open mind has been cited as a major source of discontent among the followership. So many problems can be avoided if we have an open mind. All of these traits are within reach. They are all obtainable and within reach through self-development.

Great leaders have the ability to cast their vision and to motivate others to develop their purpose. Developing others who only operate with reason is not enough for great leaders. Reason affects the mind, but purpose affects the heart. A leader's focus is to empower and align people with similar purpose. This is when incredible things begin to happen. I have a saying called the five Ps: Purposed passionate people possess power. The power I speak of is not the power to rule the world. It's the power to change the world. Your world.

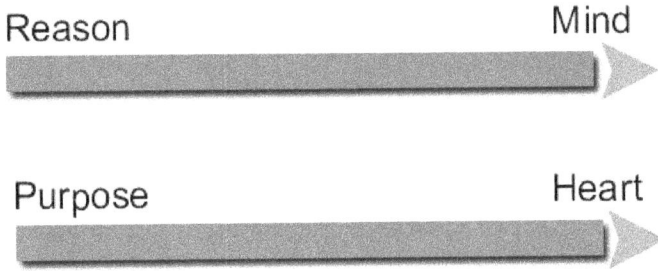

(Diagram 5.1)

Who has more desire, the follower/team member filled with reason or purpose? As we seek to develop others, we must be able to recognize the purpose filled follower. Managers give reasons, but leaders inspire purpose.

Leaders need to shift from thinking they are managing their team to the idea that they are leading the team. It is in this mental shift that you will begin to view differently the opportunities that surround you.

The United States military has long been known for the ability to develop outstanding leaders. Each branch of the U.S. military has a specific creed as to its leadership traits, but the overall variance is slight.

Marine Corps Leadership Traits (3)

- *Dependability:* The certainty of proper performance of duty.

- *Bearing:* Creating a favorable impression in carriage, appearance, and personal conduct at all times.

- *Courage:* The mental quality that recognizes fear of danger or criticism but enables a man to proceed in the face of it with calmness and firmness.

- *Decisiveness:* Ability to make decisions promptly and to announce them in clear, forceful manner.

- *Endurance:* The mental and physical stamina measured by the ability to withstand pain, fatigue, stress, and hardship.

- *Enthusiasm:* The display of sincere interest and exuberance in the performance of duty.

- *Initiative:* Taking action in the absence of orders.

- *Integrity:* Uprightness of character and soundness of moral principles; includes the qualities of truthfulness and honesty.

- *Judgment:* The ability to weigh facts and possible solutions on which to base sound decisions.

- *Justice:* Giving reward and punishment according to merits of the case in question. The ability to administer a system of rewards and punishments impartially and consistently.

- *Knowledge:* Understanding of a science or an art. The range of one's information, including professional knowledge and an understanding of your marines.

- *Tact:* The ability to deal with others without creating offense.

- *Unselfishness:* Avoidance of providing for one's own comfort and personal advancement at the expense of others.

- *Loyalty:* The quality of faithfulness to country, the corps, the unit, to one's seniors, subordinates, and peers.

When applying military leadership styles, one must recognize the unique dynamics involved with regard to the followership, the circumstances, and overall cultural environment of the military. While the core characteristics remain, the approach and delivery may need to be modified to fit the dynamics of your followership.

Are Leaders Born or Developed?

Are great leaders born or developed? The answer is yes! Some people are born with a natural compass for leadership. They find it very easy and comfortable leading people and attracting followers. However, without development, this natural ability will only go so far.

We can ask the same question about a highly skilled athlete like a quarterback. Are quarterbacks born or developed? The answer is yes. There are those who have a natural ability that makes a particular job easier, but natural ability must be developed if they are going to move past high school football, then college, and ultimately to the professional level. Once at the professional level, the player still must develop if he is going to then become an elite or "great" quarterback. It would be absurd to think you could take someone with natural ability and never give him any development, never breakdown the position, the fundamentals, how to move his feet, how to read a defense, or how to run an offense and expect him to become even a good quarterback, much less a great one. So why do we do that to people in leadership? Just because they display some natural ability of leadership doesn't mean we don't develop them and those around them. Isn't leading people far more important than playing a football game? When does the quarterback stop developing? When does the quarterback stop practicing running the offense or throwing the balls to the receivers in preparation for the game? The answer is they don't. Even though they may be at an elite level, they practice harder, and they spend more time sharpening their skills. So again I ask, why should you as a leader get comfortable and stop sharpening your skills even though you may have reached a point where you feel like you have it all figured out?

Development never stops. The great leaders come to the realization that the more they know, the more they can learn.

Chapter 6:
Personality Types

"You do not lead by hitting people over the head—
that's assault, not leadership."

Dwight Eisenhower

Personality Types

Ihave been a student of personality types for some years now. I have conducted numerous hours of research and study on this subject. I have come to learn this is a topic that can be as complicated as you make it. The goal here is to give you a basic understanding and present it in a real-life, practical application. I have taught this material in various settings and have found fancy words and drawn-out explanations just aren't practical for us everyday working leaders. I guarantee you that knowing this information will change your leadership. The ability of leaders to understand the personality types of the followers is important, but being able to style your approach to that particular person is imperative. Great leaders appreciate and seek a diverse follower base. Each personality type processes information differently, knowing how to deliver your message in a manner that is easiest for them to digest maximizes your effectiveness. In the end, we want the information to be understood and acted on; crafting it in a way that is easy for each person to accept helps ensure this.

If you have been exposed to this type of information but haven't begun to apply it, I encourage you to consider practicing it. I promise you this will be one area that you can make a quantum leadership leap.

The system uses two categories they are Expressive and Forceful. Within those categories there are two classifications; Less and More. Diagram 6.1 shows how they are arranged on a chart.

(Diagram6.1)

Let's define the headings in the chart:

• **Less or More Forceful:** The word forceful in this application has nothing to do with the physical side and everything to do with the words, demeanor, and the directness in which the person speaks and acts.

• **Less or More Expressive:** The word expressive in this application refers to how personable, easy going, open to communication and inviting the person is.

Four Basic Styles

There are four distinct personality styles; the term in boldface is one I developed for the clinical term, which is given in parenthesis. I have found these terms provide for an immediate image that helps in the understanding and ultimately the application of the knowledge. I encourage you to use whatever term you find easier to remember and associate with the character traits. The most important part is to begin immediately applying the information to your leadership.

C.P.A. (Analytical)

The C.P.A. is a well-organized individual. This person operates in a very structured environment. They crave facts and figures, and enjoys researching every possible angle. They thrive in a task-orientated culture. These individuals tend to make slower decisions and base those decisions on facts and data not personal feelings. They thrive in environments where they can use their intellect; they are deliberate and logical. Often times these individuals like to have authority. The C.P.A. avoids confrontation.

General (Driver)

The General is the person who is on the move; he gets things done and tends to be very goal driven. They dislike people who waste time and don't do their share. Generals carry themselves in a very rigid and upright manner; they tend to walk fast and always seem to be in a hurry. They love high-pressure situations. They often are viewed as offensive because of they don't make time for small talk. They are focused on results first and people are a distant second. Generals are quick to make decisions based on a fast assessment of the facts. They are decisive and assertive and are considered risk takers. Generals love authority and do not mind confrontation.

Oprah (Amiable)

The Oprah is a person who needs to connect to other people. He is into feelings and emotions, and invests heavily in personal relationships. They like to share and expect others to share with them. These individuals base their decisions on personal feeling and the ability to judge the people involved in the situation or presenting the idea. They are loyal and perceptive, and they have the ability to make decisions quickly depending on the circumstances. They tend to try to resolve any situation with all parties feeling like they have gained. They avoid confrontation.

Entertainer (Expressive)

Entertainers are always on stage. They tend to be the life of the party; they love attention and are sociable. They are "into" what others think about them and tend to invest in appearances. They base decisions on what other respected individuals think and how it will make them be viewed. Routine and structure are not important to them. They are more focused on people than tasks, and they are enthusiastic and dramatic. Generally they possess shorter attention spans and will postpone making decisions. Entertainers love authority but avoid confrontation.

Putting the four personality types on the chart gives a visual reference.

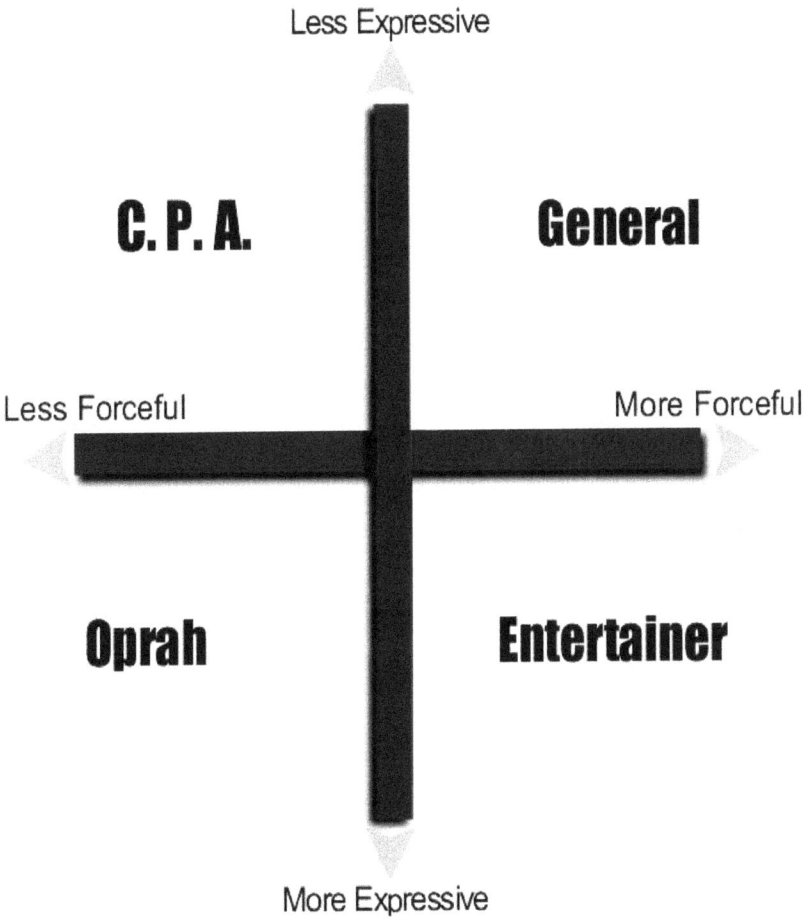

(Diagram 6.2)

By using this diagram we can see that the C.P.A. is less forceful and less expressive. The General is more forceful and less expressive.

Oprah is more expressive and less forceful, and the Entertainer is both more forceful and more expressive. By now you should be matching people in your life with these four personality styles. You might be thinking to yourself that they tend to be a combination of a few, which is absolutely correct. At different times and in different situations, you will see a shift in the personality type, however we all have a default personality type that is more dominate.

My observations, combined with my personal journey, have led me to conclude that we have the ability to rewire our default setting. With a laser-like focus and a burning desire for self-improvement we can permanently change the way we interact with people. This can change the way we lead, influence, and develop those people around us. Some of my most exciting personal growth occurred when I started analyzing the environment in which I chose to live. What I saw when I looked was my environment wasn't healthy. It was impacting my relationships in a negative way. I wasn't happy, and it was counterproductive to reaching past my personal potential. I empowered myself to change my environment and to magnify my influence, so I could develop people in a larger way. This is a choice. If you find yourself leading an environment or a culture that is counterproductive, you must act to change it. We must be vigilant in creating the best environment for both our growth and the growth of those we lead. Great leaders understand a healthy environment is paramount to the growth of an organization and the morale of the team.

For example if you are a General and you lead more Oprahs you know that they have a need to connect. However you find very little personal value in it. Whose responsibility is it to adapt and relate? It's yours as the leader. By investing time to the Oprah the connecting that they need will encourage them to increase the amount of influence you have with them.

Chapter 7:
Influence

"Influence may be the highest level of human skills."

Unknown

What Is It?

Influence: "A power affecting a person, thing, or course of events, especially one that operates without any direct or apparent effort."[1] Influence is more than the power of suggestion. Influence exists and operates in both our conscience and subconscious mind. Influence is a powerful force that can be used to accomplish great things or, as we have seen in history, to destroy.

Some of the most common examples of how influence works in our conscious mind can be found in:

- How we use our time.

- With whom we invest our time.

- With whom we choose to develop relationships.

- What we view as important and valuable.

- What we choose to do for entertainment.

- Where we get our news.

- What we read.

These are all things that we make conscious decisions about, and those decisions grant people or sources influence over our actions, thoughts, and beliefs. The subconscious mind works with the conscious mind in decision making. Your subconscious is constantly evaluating and processing your thoughts and emotions, it stores this information for later use.

When we first meet someone, or they are introduced into our life through a media outlet, we make conscious decisions about them. As we become more familiar with the person and if we have made the decision that we in fact will allow that person into our life, it moves into a subconscious state of influence. So the more familiar we become the more subconscious it becomes.

> Influence is the willingness of both the conscious and subconscious working together that allows a person to help direct or control ones actions.

Generally the closer we become and the more you respect a person, the more influence they will have in your life. This is not a conscious decision that we make such as time spent to influence ratio. Rather, as the relationship deepens our willingness to allow influence increases. Influence is not based purely on personal relationships; it is also bred in our desires and wants. Here are some common factors that produce influence.

Influence Factors

- Personal desires

- Personal wants

- Bonds and ties

- High level of respect

- Admiration

- Closeness

- Shared experiences

- Personal relationships

- Sense of right and wrong

- Similar experiences

If you have the desire to become successful and then have an opportunity to meet or become associated with a successful person, your desire would allow the already successful person a level of influence in your life. Even though there is not a relationship or closeness, your desire has paved the way for the successful person to have influence with you.

We can also look to shared experiences as an ability to produce influence. In the 1990s there was a surge in the popularity of team-building exercises for companies. Some of these exercises can be very extreme weekend retreats and some are just afternoon sessions. These events serve numerous purposes, including building shared experiences and bonds. The same is true with similar experiences; those who have something in common tend to have some level of connection and that alone can produce influence. The great leaders realize how to use these factors to increase influence.

How Do You Develop Influence?

No formula for developing influence exists; there are so many variables that it would be impossible to establish such a formula. Everybody is unique and responds differently to things. There are some common fundamental building blocks that all leaders should know to help create influence.

- Likeability

- Credibility

- Commonality

- Appearance

- How you carry yourself

- How you interact with others

- The language you use

- Influence endorsements

For most of us, a high level of influence is not created instantly; it is something that builds over a period of time. It's a process that grows as the relationship or interaction grows.

Influence Staircase

The influence staircase was created to show the levels and progression that influence takes as it is developed. There are five major steps in the staircase and each has an element of depth. How fast influence is developed and moves from one level to the next depends on the people involved. All leaders must know that once you have contact with a person, you have stepped onto that person's influence staircase. How high you step, how quickly you move, and how long you stay at each level is determined by the person's motives and the leader's ability to appeal to them. The appeal must be genuine and sincere. It is worth noting that contact can take on a lot of different forms such as person to person, articles about you, marketing pieces, and virtually any form of media can be considered contact for influence purposes.

We come into contact with various people every day. The majority of the contact will be causal encounters; even those casual encounters, regardless of how brief, have a reaction that places you on other individuals' influence staircases. Understanding this portion of the law of influence will positively affect your leadership. One person may give more influence than the other person resulting in a different step on his staircase. A successful person would have a higher level of influence with a person desiring success. In most instances, a person desiring success would have a lower level of influence with a successful person.

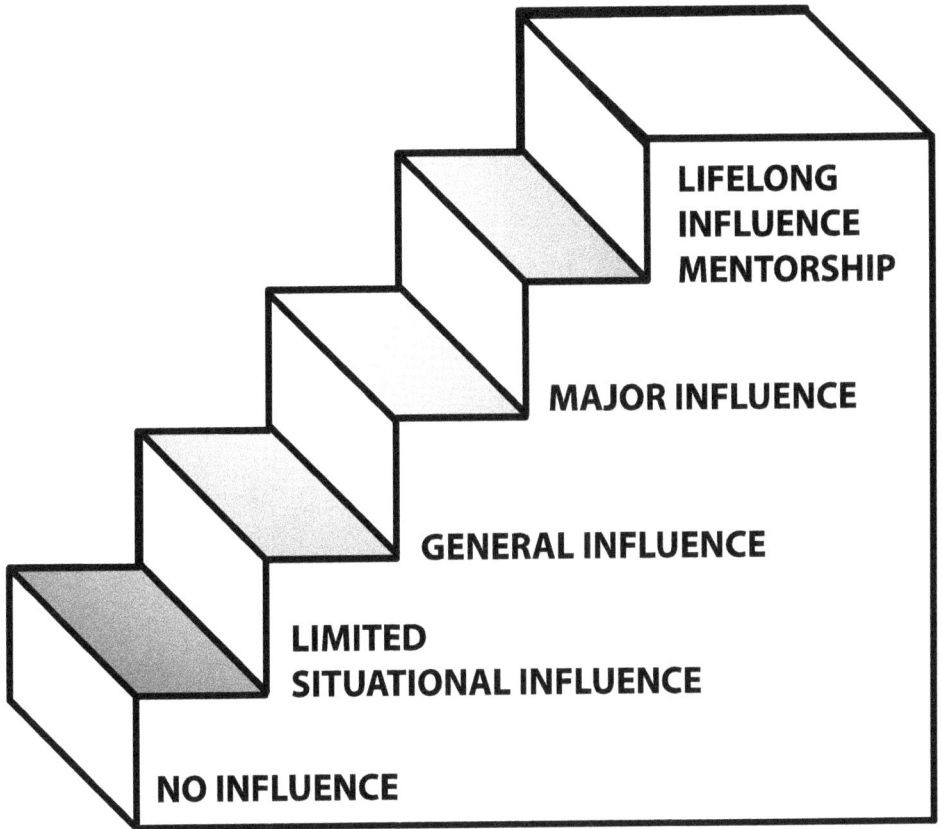

LIFELONG
INFLUENCE
MENTORSHIP

MAJOR INFLUENCE

GENERAL INFLUENCE

LIMITED
SITUATIONAL INFLUENCE

NO INFLUENCE

(Diagram 7.1)

- ## No Influence

This is the lowest level in the staircase. This is not necessarily the point that all people step onto the staircase. You cannot lead a person from this level; he must allow you to take a step up the staircase and give you some influence before he will accept your leadership. As we follow the steps outlined throughout this book, your goal will be to enter someone's staircase at the highest level possible.

- ## Limited Situational/Project Limited Influence

This is the type of influence that one may give based on a situation or a project. This is a very limited influence and generally has very little depth.

- ## General Influence

General influence is the first step that begins to develop depth. This is the level from which most leaders lead. Moving past this level requires significant work in the areas of both self-development and the development of those you lead.

- ## Major Influence

This is really the step that you start to see a change in the relationship. This is a level that the development process really shows. This is a very deep level and builds strong leader-follower relations. When your core team moves you to this level, your leadership and team are solid and strong. Most of your followership will keep you at this level but you will move deep into it.

• **Lifelong Influence Mentorship**

This is where great leaders operate. It is the deepest of all levels. The depth continues to grow in conjunction with the influence. Typically at this level a strong bond between the parties exists, and there is a personal element to the relationship.

Why Is It Important?

Without the ability to influence we would severely handicap ourselves. Everything we have has been touched by influences at some point. There is not a product made that does not have its roots in an influential element. The simple cup of coffee most of us never think about has been carefully massaged with influence from the beginning. The farmer had to be influenced to plant the coffee crop; once the beans were harvested, the farmer had to influence the distributor to purchase them. The coffee distributor influenced the coffee shop to carry that particular type of coffee, and ultimately you had to be influenced to spend the $4.00 for the cup of coffee. This is a simple illustration, but you can see how influence plays a role even in an insignificant purchase. It's the same with our leadership. Behind the scenes others are making decisions to buy-in based on the level of influence that we have with them. Leadership is based on your ability to influence. Without the gift of influence, you will not be able to lead.

Chapter 8:
Influence Endorsements and the Echo Effect

"The will to win is worthless if you do not have the will to prepare."

Thane Yost

Influence Endorsements

An influence endorsement is an endorsement given for you by another person. The influence endorsement can be either personal or professional. Influence endorsements are powerful and can be leveraged to create a higher than normal entry level on the influence staircase.

To have the most impact the influence endorsements should come from a person or source that has a level of influence with that person. Notice the words used: person or source. The endorsement need not always come from a close personal relation, it can come from any source the person has deemed creditable and has given even the slightest level of influence to. Endorsements can be either formal or informal; in fact some of the most powerful influence endorsements are informal. For example, recommending a particular movie to a friend is an informal influence endorsement. We do this throughout our day without ever considering the effect it may have. It is imperative that we understand the responsibility of leadership and strive to lead in a way that allows for positive endorsements to be produced naturally.

Influence Endorsement Forms

There are three forms of influence endorsements:

- Personal

- Action

- Source

Personal: The best influence endorsement that will ever be given is the positive spoken word. This is a proactive endorsement. There is not another form of endorsement that will give you influence faster. When an individual that has already given you a General (position 3 on the influence staircase) or higher level of influence, endorses you to another, it generates credibility for you.

Action: Action is based on the fact that others have invested in you. This is considered a proactive influence endorsement. When a person who has been given influence has invested his time, energy, effort, passion, or money in you or with your organization, this becomes an influence endorsement.

Source: A source is considered a passive endorsement. They can come from sources like the local chamber of commerce, newspaper, magazine articles, trade/industry publications, or news broadcasts. The source category is endless. Because the source is passive, it often takes more than one source to effectively create influence. This category can be leveraged to assist with building pride and confidence within the organization. People like to know that outside sources believe their leadership and the organization is worthy of honors. This builds confidence and pride among the team and can assist in achieving higher levels of influence for you with your team. This type of endorsement is extremely useful for attracting people or prospective clients.

Why Do They Work

People have a fear of making wrong decisions and being looked at as foolish. Most find an influence endorsement as a type of guarantee or security. They don't feel alone and feel a sense of protection when they have an influence endorsement. For leaders, this is beneficial when we are sharing our vision with others. Naturally, some may be apprehensive and need help with the buy-in. Having others give their endorsement allows for those people to set aside their natural fears long enough to imagine the positive possibilities rather than focusing on their fear.

Influence Echo Effect

Perhaps one of the most exciting effects that comes from an influence endorsement is the influence echo effect. This happens when the influence endorsement continues to be passed on from one individual or organization to another without the endorsement coming from the original source. This is a powerful tool to leverage in your leadership. Perhaps you have the need to influence individuals already in your organization, or you're looking to attract like purposed people. The influence echo can help you accomplish this.

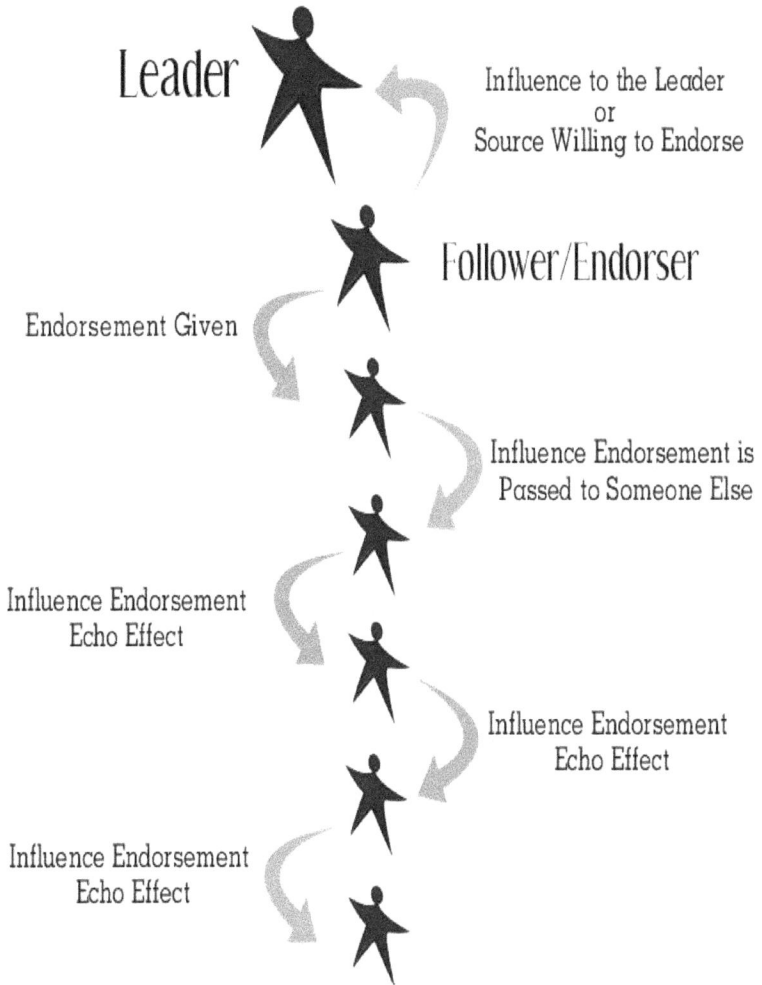

Leader

Influence to the Leader
or
Source Willing to Endorse

Follower/Endorser

Endorsement Given

Influence Endorsement is
Passed to Someone Else

Influence Endorsement
Echo Effect

Influence Endorsement
Echo Effect

Influence Endorsement
Echo Effect

(Diagram 8.1)

Influence Echo Effect and Social Media

One of the most amazing things that has happened in recent years is the development of the Internet. It has completely changed the world and the way people connect. The evolution of Facebook and other social media sites increase the power of the echo effect. The *like* button on many of these websites is another way of providing social proof that leverages endorsements. This is absolute genius and is a form of an influence endorsement with serious potential to create influence echo effects of a magnitude that has never been seen. Companies are pouring a tremendous amount of money to bump up the likes on their web sites. Why does it matter? The premise is, if your friends and family like something, try their product. Even if no one you know has liked a particular product or person, the fact that 10,000 others have provides a tremendous influence endorsement resulting in a very loud echo effect. Leadership comes down to these same principles. Of course it is not a button on a website that makes a great leader. However, it is using this concept of conducting your life and leadership in a way that others will naturally want to give you these endorsements that creates a powerful echo effect. Social proof is a stamp of approval for the new generation; the echo effect leverages this social proof.

Chapter 9:
Power Types

"The quality of a leader is reflected in the standards they set for themselves."

Ray Kroc

Rigid, Flexible, and Passive Power

T here are three power systems that can be used to accomplish goals and affect people. They are rigid power, passive power, and flexible power. Each one has some common elements, however, there is one that great leaders use to build a strong and passionate team.

Rigid Power:

Rigid power is stiff; it's hard and not malleable. Rigid power operates on fear and intimidation to accomplish goals. Rigid power is often viewed as oppressive and can create a stressful work environment. Rigid power has a limiting element because it only effects the physical actions of a person. Lasting change is hard to accomplish with rigid power because it operates on the principle that there will be punishment for not complying. It's a fear-based power structure. For rigid power to be effective there must be components of threats, enforcement, and severe punishment. There is always a feeling that someone or thing is watching to catch a violation of a rule or regulation. Once a violation has happened swift and harsh punishment must occur, or it loses its power. Seeking of violations is not to uphold high standards; it is to hold power over a person or group. Rigid power is not concerned with willingness or cooperation because it uses the enforcement component to accomplish its goals. New managers and those leaders with low self-worth fall prey to Rigid Power Syndrome.

Rigid Power Syndrome occurs when threats and fear are used as the primary form of motivation for workers to complete tasks. Those suffering from Rigid Power Syndrome will use phrases that make it known that they are "the boss" and they are in charge. They enjoy using the power card of "I'll have you fired if you don't" or a hybrid of that phrase. Those who choose to use rigid power tend to have a workplace with high turnover of employees, low morale, a negative environment, and a culture of everyone for themselves. It is nearly impossible to have a team concept that thrives under these conditions. Stress is bred at an unmanageable rate, multiplying with each hour worked. These types of leaders rarely move beyond the point of limited/project influence (position two) on the influence staircase.

Passive Power:

Passive power is nonthreatening and has a submissive feel. Passive power relies on the individual's conscience and sense of duty to perform to expectations. Enforcement of standards and expectations occur only in extreme cases and as a last resort. Passive power is a breeding ground for frustration because of the lack of consistency. The leader who uses passive power is consumed with making everyone feel good and works hard to avoid any type of confrontation. The unwillingness to confront individuals leads those with more dominant personalities to exploit the passive-power structure. Those individuals with low work ethic take advantage of the non-enforcement of standards and mediocrity spreads throughout the organization at warp speed. Passive power leads to a collapse of the organization, and the followers are leaderless.

Flexible Power:

Flexible power is firm but pliable and relies on personal buy-in and cooperation from those you lead. Flexible power tends to breed lasting change because of the buy-in factor involved. Flexible power must gain the cooperation and genuine willingness of those involved to accomplish the goal. Flexible power uses the uniqueness of each person and situation to produce the highest level of results. Those leaders who use flexible power generally enjoy a high level of respect and trust from the followership. Flexible power produces a higher level of influence and allows the leader to move higher on the influence staircase of the followership. The key is to understand that flexible power is versatile and can adapt to any follower or leadership challenge.

> "It is the nature of man to rise to greatness if greatness is expected of him."
>
> -John Steinbeck

The danger in flexible power is not using the firm element of this structure. Many leaders use a diluted form of flexible power leaving out this key component. They embrace the portions of cooperation and using individual's personalities to motivate, but fail to enforce the standards and expectations. They are afraid to be firm with people; they suddenly shift to passive power when it comes to confronting issues. Failure to confront and enforce standards results in not having standards, and ultimately it erodes leadership and undermines the organizations viability. This puts the entire organization at risk. Flexible power needs to have the firm element to make it work effectively. Failing to adhere to this principle will cause confusion and a sense of lack of control.

Flexible power at its core is being open, aware, alert, and educated enough to identify that each individual or situation is different and that to be effective, your leadership needs to be appropriate. Great leaders know and understand the leverage of flexible power. They use this leverage to develop a high level of influence. Remember in most cases we want to develop a long lasting level of influence with those we lead. Flexible power is the way to develop this level of influence.

Fill vs. Feel Philosophy

The fill vs. feel philosophy begins with you. In essence it is the way you approach your leadership. Your team will take on which ever of these philosophies that you embrace. You will create a culture and the expectations will be set. This is one of the areas where those you lead will understand your commitment. The fill vs. feel philosophy can be one of the major differences between prepared organizations and those that are not.

Most people are moved into leadership by promotion. This isn't necessarily a bad thing. However, the criteria for the promotion is often misguided. It tends to be based on work skills, seniority, or politics. This can lead to major issues. They are filling a position. The fill in the philosophy means just that: there is a void, and they are filling the space. This is one of the absolute worst things that any leader can allow to happen in the organization they serve. This philosophy starts at the top. It is impossible to have great leaders that merely fill a leadership role.

During my years in law enforcement this seemed to be the trend. Sure, there would be a test and perhaps an oral interview based on technical work aspects such as the proper form to be completed per a particular incident. There was a lot of weight given to seniority and your likeability with the command staff. Very rarely was there anything to do with leadership, leadership development, or the true desire to lead verses the desire to move your career up the ranks and perhaps to a higher pay grade. So you are left with people filling roles and believing that they possess the skills necessary to be effective. Years of this practice breeds a culture that is toxic. Ultimately it leads to a huge gap in leaders, and the organization implodes. We must recognize that you can appoint managers, but leaders are developed.

The difference in the feel is the motivation with which the leader approaches the position. It's the mind-set, and it's the end results. It's the servant's attitude to leading. Great leaders always possess the feel approach. Remember great leaders must have a high level of influence. There is a tremendous amount of responsibility that comes with any leadership

> You cannot allow yourself to be held hostage by the fear that you must be perfect.

endeavor. When you feel it, it takes on a whole new level. You become engaged in ways that those who are filling never do. This high level of engagement becomes projected to those who you lead. The result is they increase their buy-in. Increased buy-in increases motivation and morale. This in turn results in a higher and deeper level of influence they give to you, which moves you closer to reaching your goals.

How do you approach your leadership role? Are you just moving up the ladder and looking for the next big thing? Do those who follow you believe that you are just filling the role? What do your actions show? Those who are filling are rarely concerned about becoming a great leader or moving relationships up and deep on the influence staircase. They assume their time is limited, so they don't invest in their leadership. In other words, they don't feel their leadership. Those who are feeling are constantly investing in those who follow.

Leadership Decisions: When Two Equals One

You have two choices in respect to decisions—make a decision or not make a decision. However, the reality is you only have one. Every time you decide to not make a decision you have just made one, and these decisions have consequences—often major consequences. Too many times leaders fail to grasp this simple concept and believe if they ignore an issue, it will mysteriously self-correct. This rarely happens, and if by chance it does, it takes longer and costs more. More often than not the reasons leaders fail to act is that they are afraid of hurting someone's feelings, they fear not being liked and they fear making the wrong decision. Great leaders are never malicious or reckless with respect to hurting people's feelings; however, at some point in your leadership, you are going to hurt someone's feelings. Believe it or not, you may not always be liked and upon occasion you will make mistakes. It will happen there is no way to avoid it. You can minimize those effects by the way you present yourself and the process in which you make decisions. This unattainable standard of never upsetting people or making a mistake will paralyze you and will render your leadership completely ineffective. Great leaders are not perfect. They have learned to leverage their experience and self-development to achieve higher results with more people in more circumstances. Don't fear decisions; embrace them for what they are and lead your team. This is what they are expecting and deserve.

Leadership Test

Leadership inherently has a lot to do with making decisions. Many times those decisions are ones that others would not be comfortable making. Obviously to become a great leader you must become comfortable with making decisions.

I tend to make quick decisions; I struggled with taking the time to walk through a consistent formula for making decisions. I relied heavily on logic and my instincts for making both big and small decisions. Even though for the most part I have made the correct choices, instincts and logic are not part of a transferable system that a leader can use to develop others. I learned from my good friend, Jim Ring the benefits of slowing down and working through a consistent series of questions. Doing this helps ensure all decisions are the best you are capable of making. It also provides a platform for the development of others. Jim developed these skills in me, and today I'm a much better leader as a result of the time he invested in me. I will caution you to not take more time than necessary to move through this process. Just as there is a danger in being too quick to respond, there is also danger in being too slow to respond.

Regardless of the complexity and severity of the circumstance, you should begin to use a decision-making formula. If you're not currently using a system, I encourage you to give this some thought. It is simple and consists of four basic questions that stimulate a focused thought. It's through this focused thought that ultimately helps us arrive at the best decision. Another benefit of having a system in place is that your team will know the information they will need to provide you when approaching you with a decision to be made. This is a great way to develop your team and gives you powerful insight into their ability to arrive at decisions.

1.   What is important?

2.   What are the actions to be taken?

3.   What are the costs?

4.   What are the effects?

What Is Important?

This question serves as a way to identify the goal or desired outcome. When you have not identified clearly what is important then it can lead to confusion and can sidetrack the objective. When making a decision that is a result of a problem, often we are caught in a game of who's right and who's wrong. This tends to be personal and it is always best to move as quickly away from this as possible. We need to focus on what is really important. When you can identify that you will begin to get everybody involved on the same page. Not only will it speed up the process, it will make it much smoother, too.

What Are the Actions To Be Taken?

Identifying options that could be taken is a must. There may be legal concerns or other sensitive issues that can limit the options that are available. It's imperative you know what actions you can take so you will be able to correctly evaluate those options with the two remaining questions to come to the best decision.

What Are the Costs?

This on the surface sounds like a pretty easy question, but it goes much deeper than dollars and cents. Sure the financial cost is relevant in some decisions. I want to know what the human capital costs are. What are the followership costs, the time costs, the emotional costs, what are the momentum costs, as well as the opportunity costs? Some of these can't be easily measured. Of course there are many other cost factors that are associated with particular situations, your goal is to know them.

What Are the Effects?

We as leaders need to know the effects on the organization, on our followership, on our capital, and on the potential to reach our goals. Obviously, when we can figure out the cost and then look at the effects, we can make good leadership decisions. This process doesn't have to take place in a boardroom during a two-hour meeting. This process can take seconds or minutes. As long as you have gone through the process, you should make the decision as quickly as you can.

If you struggle with decision making, having a proven system to walk you through the process will increase your comfort and ultimately your confidence. To become a great leader requires you to become a great decision maker. Becoming a great decision maker comes with making a lot of decisions. You shouldn't approach a decision with fear that you will make a mistake. But rather approach the decision as an opportunity.

Three Words to Lead By

A lot of people struggle with finding a proper balance in their professional dealings with others. I adopted three words of wisdom I learned from one of the law enforcement academies with which I participated. These three words have served me well; Firm, Fair, and Consistent.

Firm: This is an area that can be problematic if not fully understood. Firm is not being insensitive; it's not painting things in black and white only. Firm is not allowing others to use personal relationships to interfere with making correct decisions that benefit the majority. However, firm is being clear as to purpose and goals. Firm is being uncompromised as to your conviction in your purpose. Firm is not allowing a culture of laziness to be bred. It is holding yourself and others to a high set of standards and expectations. Firm is not oppressive. Firm is objective.

Fair: Is just as it sounds. It's being fair to others and yourself. It's being ethical and trustworthy in your dealings. While you will make decisions that won't be popular with everyone, if you are known for making fair decisions, they will be accepted with minimal disruption. With that being said, fair doesn't mean everything is divided evenly like you would if you were dealing with children. Fair is making the right decision based on the facts and not personal relationships.

Consistent: Consistency is stability for most people and it is the reassurance that there is a system that is dependable predictable. I have been involved in organizations that the only thing that was consistent was the lack of consistency. I cannot begin to describe to you the frustration and doubt this creates. Consistency is a must for all great leaders. Consistency equals dependability and a level of security. If you want to grow your influence and your team you must be consistent.

Abraham Lincoln is known for being one of the greatest leaders the United States of America has ever had. Few can measure up to his leadership skills. Those skills are on display in the form of a letter that President Lincoln wrote to the newly appointed General Hooker.

President Lincoln had met with the general to discuss his expectations for the war effort, as well as the general's behavior issues. General Hooker had been known for his vocal criticism for his former commanding officers. General Hooker had even gone as far as to say what the country needed was a dictator. This behavior did not set well with President Lincoln, and he knew he needed to address it. In addition to addressing it in person during their meeting, he gave the general a letter as the meeting concluded. As you read the letter I want you to think in terms of three thoughts introduced in this chapter. Think about the three power systems; rigid, passive and flexible power, of the fill vs. feel philosophy, and lastly of the words, firm, fair, and consistent.

Here is the letter to General Hooker from President Abraham Lincoln.(1)

Executive Mansion

Washington, January 26, 1863

Major General Hooker:

General.

I have placed you at the head of the Army of the Potomac. Of course, I have done this upon what appears to me to be sufficient reasons. And yet I think it best for you to know that there are some things in regard to which, I am not quite satisfied with you. I believe you to be a brave and skillful soldier, which, of course, I like. I also believe you do not mix politics with your profession, in which you are right. You have confidence in yourself, which is valuable, if not an indispensible quality. You are ambitious, which, with in reasonable bounds, does good rather than harm. But I think that during Gen. Burnside's command of the Army, you have taken counsel of your ambition, and thwarted him as much as you could, in which you did a great wrong to the country, and to a most meritorious and honorable brother officer. I have heard, in such a way as to believe it, of your recently saying that both the Army and the Government needed a Dictator. Of course it was not for this, but in spite of it, that I have given you the command. Only those generals who gain successes, can set up dictators. What I now ask of you is military success, and I will risk the dictatorship. The government will support you to the upmost of its ability, which is neither more nor less than it has done and will do for all commanders. I much fear that the spirit which you have aided to infuse into the

Army, of criticizing their Commander, and withholding confidence from him, will not turn upon you. I shall assist you as far as I can, to put it down. Neither you, nor Napoleon, if he were alive again, could get any good out of an army, while such a spirit prevails in it.

And now, beware of rashness. Beware of rashness, but with energy, and sleepless vigilance, go forward, and give us victories.

Yours very truly

A. Lincoln

This letter displays the best in the philosophies outlined in this chapter. These 351 words echo his genuine and purpose-driven leadership. He set forth his vision and expectations and allowed the general to buy-in. He is straightforward and clear yet not condescending. He is firm, fair, and consistent, and yet he is able to apply the principle of flexible power. There is no doubt that the president felt the position and wasn't just filling it. He needed the general to do the same. President Lincoln gives the general the direction in which to go but lets him choose the path to get there. His admonishments are accompanied by his support. He gives General Hooker a new reputation to live up to—one of military success. He closes the letter with a highly motivational tone telling him to "Beware of rashness, but with energy, and sleepless vigilance, go forward, and give us victories." The president embodies the essence of a great leader. He knew that words were powerful and understood properly placed words can magnify that power.

Chapter 10:
Communication

"The way we communicate with others and with ourselves ultimately determines the quality of our lives."

Anthony Robbins

Communication

As babies we communicated our needs for food by loud sounds; those sounds were interpreted as our need to be fed and we received food. Communication at its core is a survival technique. We think in terms of words when we think of communication, but communication reaches far beyond words. Communication encompasses verbal, verbal tone, and nonverbal behavior. There have been many articles and books written on the percentages associated with each. Regardless of what the actual percentages may be, it is important to understand that communication includes all three. Those with whom we communicate are responding to more than just the words that we are using.

Visual

Today more than ever those with whom we communicate expect to have visual stimulus. We have become a visually stimulated society. With the advancement of technology and its functions in our everyday life, people have come to expect a visual component to communication. Whether it's in an electronic form (video or slide presentation) or your body language, people are keyed into visual stimuli.

Words

Words are powerful whether written or spoken. Words have the ability to be constructive or destructive. Great leaders are the ones who have developed the skill to use their words so that they will be constructive. Leaders who use this skill are constantly building others up. Your past words lay the foundation for the words of today and tomorrow. Leaders who recklessly mix constructive and destructive words are constantly tearing down the progress they may have made in the past.

Regardless of the situation, your words should be constructive. Some leaders are good at using constructive words while engaged in a professional situation but use destructive words in a relaxed setting. I cringe at the thought of how I have been guilty of this in the past. I had always been aware that while in a counseling session I needed to use constructive words and phrases, and I always tried to leave the session with a positive tone. However while walking through the office or in more casual settings, I would use destructive words as a source of humor. Never taking into consideration that my words were destructive and counterproductive to the goals I was trying to reach. One incident is bad enough but making this a pattern is destructive in many ways. As leaders we need to be aware of our words in all settings and use our words in a constructive manner always seeking to build and develop others.

> Life depends on communication. The ability to communicate is something we begin to learn from the moment we are born.

Attention

One of the most difficult things for busy leaders to do is give their full attention to the person when communicating. Being present both physically and mentally is paramount when communicating. This combined with active listening is perhaps the two largest areas that we can immediately improve on, allowing us to increase our ability to communicate. How many times have we been guilty of shuffling papers or working on the computer when others are attempting to engage us? It's disrespectful and it conveys to the other person that they aren't important. Begin to make an effort to give your full attention when communicating.

Ethos, Logos, and Pathos

In the book Rhetoric, Aristotle describes the art of persuasion as being rooted in three things: ethos, logos, and pathos.[1]

Ethos: Describes the credibility of the speaker or writer. We believe those we find to be creditable and respect. People who have reached certain levels of success we tend to view as an authority and give them expert status. This results in a level of influence that creates a desire to listen.

Logos: Is the logic used to present the material. Any communication in which you are attempting to persuade or convince must have a logical base.

Pathos: Is the appeal to the emotions of the person with whom you are communicating. It can also be interpreted as the passion with which you present the material that creates emotion.

All of these communication elements are essential to gaining influence. Moving up the influence staircase is necessary for leaders. The inability to effectively communicate with others will limit your ability to reach your goals. Leaders need to be able to communicate with different people on different levels. Your communication must be flexible. Too many times we find those who communicate on their level and expect you to be flexible enough to meet that style. As leaders, we need to be the ones that modify our style to meet those with whom we are communicating. As we discussed in Chapter 6 knowing the personality styles will help do just that.

You can dramatically improve your communication by improving your listening skills. Good listening is a major step to good communication. Generally most people never take the time to develop these skills; we are taught to always have the final word and that we should be a step ahead of others. I believe when it comes to communication the last word isn't important, and instead of being one step ahead, we should strive to be in step. Here are some action steps you can take to improve your communication and ultimately to improve the way you connect with others.

1.   **Listen**

Aggressively listening to the other person means that you are attempt-ing to capture every word and thought. Typically we listen to about every other word and prepare for what we are going to say. Listening does take practice and concentration. However the rewards for listening are great.

2.   Use the person's name

Dale Carnegie in his masterpiece book "How to Win Friends and Influence People" says, "remember that a person's name is to that person the sweetest and most important sound in any language." Making the effort to remember someone's name makes an impact on that person and shows you have an interest in them.

3.   Ask questions

Asking questions builds dialogue and helps keep the person talking. The questions should be open ended and center on the person or topic. An open-ended question is a question that cannot be answered with just a yes or no. People enjoy talking about themselves so let them. Ask questions to keep them talking.

4.   Use encouraging statements

Using encouraging statements gives them permission to continue talking. Encouraging statements include, tell me more, go on, I'd like to hear more, that's interesting, and that's fantastic.

5.   Keep an open body posture

Keeping an open body posture will encourage the conversation. You should avoid crossing your arms or taking any body position that could be interpreted as closed or uninterested. Leaning forward slightly and nodding your head are good encouraging gestures that show you are engaged. Using the mirror technique has also proven to be effective; in this technique you mirror the image of the person with whom you are speaking. For example, if he moves his left hand to illustrate a point, you would use your right hand on a delay and in a smaller movement. When he moves his body position, you would move your body position. The key is the movements should be delayed and slight. When preformed properly the mirror technique builds rapport without the other person noticing your movements.

6.   Eye contact

There are some cultures where making eye contact is a form of disrespect. However for most western cultures it is a must for building trust. In the book "First Things First" Kurt and Brenda Warner explain a rule that they have to teach their kids the importance of eye contact.(2) When they are eating out at a restaurant their children must be able to tell them what color eyes the server has. This is teaching them to always look people in the eye and to value them. Making firm eye contact is a must for leaders. Practice the Warner's rule with yourself. Do you know the color of eyes of the people who are on your team?

7.   Don't interrupt

Interrupting is a sign of disrespect. It shows the other person that you don't care enough about their thought, view, or idea to let them express it. Let them finish the thought give them the respect to express themselves.

8.   Be sincere

You can't fake sincerity nor should you ever try. Be sincere or don't bother engaging in the conversation. People will sense insincerity quickly, and this will damage the relationship.

9.   Thirty-second rule

In the book "Twenty-Five Ways to Win with People" the authors John Maxwell and Less Parrott explain the principle of the thirty-second rule. "Within thirty seconds of a conversation, say something encouraging to a person."(3) I have found this to be one of the most dynamic tools I use. I have physically seen faces light up and body posture straighten by a few well-chosen words. I always leave feeling more encouraged myself. That's the magic behind it, the more you give, the more you receive.

10.   Make the other person feel important

We all have the need to feel important. Give the other person your attention. Make them feel like they are the only person in the room. Give them the benefit of your full attention.

11.   Stay positive

Don't complain or be dragged down the road of negativity. Stay away from comments that are negative about others. Stay positive because there is power in positivity.

12.   Smile

Your smile is one of the most powerful tools you have. People are attracted to people that smile. Others perceive a smile as warm, happy, confident, and trustworthy. Smiling disarms people and warms them up. Who would you rather be around someone who smiles or someone who always wears a frown?

Written Communications

E-mail and other technology has allowed for faster and greater written communication. We live in a society of information overload. As leaders, we need to be aware of this and send out information in a clear and concise manner. Whenever possible be brief and use bullet points. The clearer you can make the message, the more effective it will be.

Use caution when sending messages that aren't purpose related. Online jokes and chain letters send the wrong message to your team. Your actions encourage others. You will find by engaging in that type of activity you will encourage others to do so as well. A recent survey revealed that 22 percent of workers wasted two hours of their workday and 14 percent stated that they wasted three hours of their workday. The most common reason (48 percent) was Internet use.(4) As leaders, we cannot develop others to reach past their potential and reach our goals if we encourage this type of behavior.

Meetings

Meetings have the potential to waste time and resources. Meetings are necessary and should occur, but all meetings should follow an agenda to ensure that the time invested is producing results. The best practice for meetings is to have an agenda typed and distributed to all partici-pants to help maintain structure. You should encourage openness in your meetings, but you must stay focused and on topic. In addition there should be a person designated to take clear and concise notes. Meetings should never be longer than they have to be; the goal should always be to maximize the time. All meetings should begin and end the same. You should always begin with an introduction and end with a motivational statement.

Public Speaking/S.E.C.T.I.O.N. Formula

It was during my law enforcement career I began to notice that my public speaking skills were not where I wanted them to be. At that point I had not had any development courses on the subject and relied heavily on what I happened to pick up listening to other speakers. I was in a command staff meeting when the chief requested research on a specific certified traffic school class. I volunteered to oversee the project and within a few weeks I presented the findings. The decision was made that we would move forward with the program but that we needed someone to instruct the four hour-long class. I knew there was no one excited about teaching the class and typically it would have been "forced" onto a new officer. I volunteered for the assignment knowing it would give me the opportunity to develop my speaking skills and spare the officers from something they viewed as a waste of time. I instructed that class for over two years. Those attending the class were there by court mandate and on top of that the class cost over $100.00. The ages of people in the class ranged from sixteen to ninety, and the material to be taught would be considered by most painfully dry. I knew that the skills I would have to develop would serve me well.

The first few classes I stuck to the course outline that was prepared by the company certifying the class. This was torture for both the participants and myself. Halfway through the third class, I closed the notebook, sat on the edge of the table, and began to relate personal stories of incidents that followed the course material. Something magical happened. They began to pay attention, they asked questions, and they became engaged. From that moment on, I understood the power of a story. Something that was dry became fun; it became interesting, and it became emotional. Most important was they were leaving with the message that I wanted them to have. I wanted to understand what was happening within this class, and this is the formula that developed itself as a result. I have used it ever since. It's called the S.E.C.T.I.O.N.

S = *Stories*: Tell stories not just facts.

E = *Emotion:* Stories told with emotion will create emotion in those who hear them.

C = *Connect:* Stories allow you to connect quickly.

T = *Trust:* Stories build trust faster than facts.

I = *Interest:* Stories are more interesting than facts alone

O = *Objective:* Stories will allow you to reach the objective faster.

N = *Never Forgotten:* Stories told with emotion are not forgotten.

Your stories should range the full spectrum of the emotional scale. From funny to sad, happy to angry, they are all available for you to use. Don't limit yourself. Learn to leverage those feelings to maximize your effect.

There will be a time in every leader's career that he will have to give some type of public speech. A lot of people have a strong fear of public speaking. If this is the case for you, you will never conquer that fear unless you develop the skill of public speaking. By not developing it, you will severely limit your opportunities. There are many times that a leader will be able to further his cause or strengthen his followership by giving a public address. If you are not prepared for such an event, then you will push those opportunities away from you. Don't miss the opportunity to advance your leadership and reach past your potential. There are many local organizations such as Toastmasters International that will help you develop these skills.

Chapter 11:
Motivation and Inspiration

"Leadership is based on a spiritual quality; the power
to inspire others to follow."

Vincent Lombardi

Motivation

A s a leader, one of the toughest challenges is to motivate an unmotivated team. The great leaders know it is easier to keep motivational momentum than to try to create it. Therefore, it is imperative that you keep connected and don't let yourself become disengaged. Even the best leaders often find themselves in difficult positions involving low morale and motivation. Perhaps you are taking over a team with low morale or worse yet; your leadership style has damaged morale. I once had a client that had a sign in the lunchroom that read, THE FIRINGS WILL CONTINUE UNTIL MORALE IMPROVES. I'm sure that he meant it as a joke but what did it say to his team? Anytime you find yourself in this position, you need to take immediate action to address it. Your first step is to identify the core problem. Too many times we focus on spin-off problems that will never address the core problem. You must invest your energy and concentration on the core problem. When the core problem is resolved, you will likely find that the spin-off problems have been resolved as well.

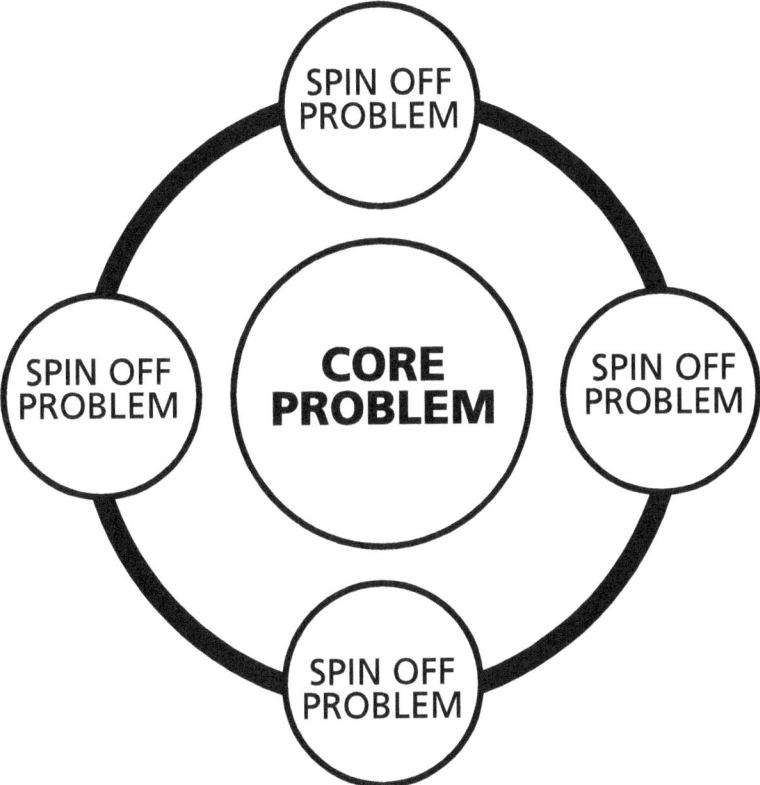

(Diagram 11.1)

Core problems can generally be classified into two categories: People and Conditions.

People

- Leadership team
- Lack of communication
- Lack of direction
- Lack of appreciation

Conditions

- Facility
- Hours
- Safety
- Overall conditions/environment

If you have problems that are not corrected then it is a leadership problem. All problems or issues will ultimately become viewed as a problem with leadership if not corrected. This is another reason why staying connected is so important. The list is not intended to represent all the possibilities but to give you a generalization of how to classify core problems.

I have seen organizations where the general mood had gotten so bad that it was US vs. THEM. Core problems left alone will breed this negative culture. This is one of the most dangerous environments that threaten the goals of any organization. I stated earlier that leaders are in the people business. You will never succeed in leadership when the culture and mood is US vs. THEM. It is impossible. I have known "leaders" who foster this culture on purpose. That is ridiculous! You will only win in leadership when you win with people. You will only win with people when you serve them.

Common Myths About Motivation

How many of these myths do you believe?

1. Money is the best motivator.

2. Threats boost morale.

3. If I leave it alone, it will go away.

4. If I let them know how lucky they are to have a job, they will see it my way.

5. Everyone is motivated by the same things.

These are just a few; we could fill a book full of misconceptions about motivation. A closer examination of each one listed will reveal the reality of the myth.

Money is the best motivator:

This couldn't be further from the truth; money is a short-term motivator, and it certainly not the best motivator. We all know that the reality of life is most people's expenses rise in direct proportion to their income. That is a fancy way of saying that the more you make, the more you'll spend. So the extra money used to "motivate" soon becomes the person's base wage. When it's in the extra stage, it does have a motivating effect. As it slips into the base stage it becomes viewed as the person's worth and is viewed as an expectation. Once viewed as an expectation the person expects to earn that amount of money regardless of where they work or how they perform their job duties. Once it reaches that point, it has lost nearly all motivational effects it had. Obviously from a capital perspective, this would be fiscally irresponsible way to use that resource. So it just doesn't work. It doesn't work for the one needing to be motivated and it doesn't work for the one wanting to motivate.

Threats boost morale:

Negative threats do not produce positive results. The insecure leader who has yet to develop solid skills will use this tactic. He views low morale as a personal attack. Lacking in leadership maturity he does not understand that this is a leadership opportunity. The mature leader seizes the opportunity and uses it for the growth of all involved.

If I leave it alone, it will go away:

Think of all the problems in the world, hunger, disease, and abuse. Do those problems seem to disappear because we ignore them? Apply the same logic to the motivation issue. It doesn't happen for the world's problems, and it will not happen for your organization's problems either. This is another favorite tactic of the insecure leader. He is so fearful in many cases that he might upset someone in the process of correcting the core problem that he convinces himself that things will improve without his involvement.

If I let them know how lucky they are to have a job, they will see things my way:

There is a lot wrong with this statement. First and foremost, this myth is approaching it with a view that he is right and that the other person is in error. The underlying theme is that it has to be his way. Again you are in the people business. The effective leader understands that he must be able to view issues from all sides.

Everyone is motivated by the same things:

If that were the case, then we wouldn't have a need for any further discussion. The fact of the matter is, there are some common needs and desires that are fairly universal in all of our lives. The key is identifying these needs and desires then providing the arena for them to be met. In her book "Get Motivated" Tamara Lowe explains that everyone has specific DNA regarding motivation. She breaks it down into three categories: drives, needs, and awards. She states that within the drives category, we have connection or production drives, within the needs category, we have stability or variety, and finally under awards, there are internal and external.(1) In over twenty years of leadership experience, I have found that if I concentrate on ten key areas that I will be successful in motivating people. Here are the ten need areas that I focus on.

10 "Need" Areas to Focus On

- Need to feel appreciated

- Need to feel important

- Need to contribute

- Need to have a sense of belonging

- Need to connect with people

- Need to be wanted

- Need to be accepted

- Need to have the opportunity to excel

- Need to know that they matter

- Need to know that you care

Some years ago I attended a seminar with my good friend Jim Ring. The seminar produced a thought that has stuck with me all of these years. The speaker said, "If your staff feels underappreciated, they will always feel underpaid." I have found truth in this statement on both levels. That of the staff and that of the leader who failed to appreciate. I have made it a point in my leadership endeavors to find ways to appreciate those whom I lead. It's worth noting that this requires you to think outside of the box, but I encourage you to never miss a chance to appreciate those you lead.

Here are some simple ways that you can show your appreciation to people.

- **A handwritten note**

The power contained in a two-sentence handwritten note is amazing. This can motivate people for years. Don't underestimate the message this conveys to people.

- **A letter to a spouse or loved one**

Writing a letter to the team members spouse or loved one telling them of the value their spouse brings to the organization is powerful. If there has been a recent accomplishment let them know how grateful you are to have them on the team and that they should be proud of them. This type of letter accomplishes a number of things. As humans we want the people we love to be proud of us, and we want them to know we bring value. Often times our work brings challenges at home from the hours or the travel involved. This letter gives a boost of motivation and often will strengthen the support at home. Don't underestimate the impact of sincere written words to the people who are important in lives of your team.

- **Public recognition**

Recognition in front of a person's peers shows that you know the value they bring. It conveys a sense of caring and serves to motive others by appealing to the desire for recognition as well.

- **Plaques** (for any legitimate reason)

Plaques are the equivalent to a trophy. When you were a child and won a trophy, you cherished it and displayed it for all to see. The same principles apply for plaques. Giving a plaque commemorates the occasion forever. It's critical to understand that the presentation of the plaque is important. When possible you as the leader should present the plaque. It doesn't have to be a formal ceremony, but it needs to be framed as a special moment. If you cannot present the plaque, the importance of the presentation moment must be conveyed to the presenter; it cannot merely be stuck in the recipient's in box. If the proper steps are not taken, you will devalue the plaque, and it will not provide the value it was designed to convey and could lead to a negative experience.

Generally the plaque will be hung on the wall of an office or at home, and every time someone comments on the plaque, the person will feel a new burst of pride. So take the steps necessary to ensure the value.

- **A sincere thank you**

It's so simple yet so often we as leaders forget to say thank you. The combination of these two words spoken with sincerity can give a person a tremendous sense of reward.

- **Unexpected gift**

A gift certificate for two for a lunch or dinner will produce motivation. It should always be for two and not one; it will produce stronger motivation because the individual will at some point make reference to the meal being a gift from the leader. Every time the person speaks these words he is creating positive feelings for you and his position within the organization. Having another person along will reinforce those feelings with positive comments for him and you.

- **A few hours off**

Most people enjoy a few unexpected hours to get an early start to a weekend. Generally speaking most production slows down Friday afternoons, so from a cost-allocation stand point, it's a good time for you and since they are already thinking of the weekend it's a good time for them. This is a great way to maximize the experience for all involved.

- **Lunches**

Eating with people is a good way to bond. Make it a point to share a meal with the team as often as you can. Typically most leaders will only have lunches with the team around the expected holidays. Make it a point to do this throughout the year. These events are only limited by your own creativity. They can be themed lunches, and you can encourage all to participate by bringing their favorite dish. Think outside the box; there is not a need to always have these events professionally catered.

These are all very affordable ways to motivate and some cost absolutely nothing. It takes some effort on the part of the leader however I guarantee the return will be enormous. In the words of Jim Rohn, "Words do two major things: They provide food for the mind and create light for understanding and awareness."

Motivation or Inspiration

The ability to motivate is a tool that all leaders need to possess. However the truly great leaders understand the significance of the ability to inspire as well. Motivation operates in the mind, using reasoning and the person's wants and desires. Inspiration operates in the heart and provokes powerful emotions and feelings.

Motivation is like a campfire that you must add fuel and tend to constantly, or it will go out. Inspiration is a forest fire that finds its own fuel and takes on a life all its own. When the leader taps into the emotional/spiritual elements of the followership through inspiration, it provides the spark that ignites this intense fire.

How Do You Inspire?

Inspiration is organic and follows no set formula. It is a culmination of a number of elements to create a synergistic effect. When the leader becomes purposed, healthy, and determined, and seeks to develop others adding value to their life, inspiration comes naturally. This is because your words, actions, convictions, character, and beliefs are all supporting your purpose. This allows your vision to have life. Consider the story of Nancy G. Brinker. As Nancy's sister Susan was ending her three-year fight with breast cancer, she made a promise to her that she would do everything in her power to end breast cancer. Susan passed away, but the promise Nancy made lives on. The creation of the Susan G. Komen for the Cure is that promise. The organization has raised over 1.5 billion dollars since its inception in 1982 and has over 1 million volunteers that support events throughout the year.(2) They have provided hope and support for those who have been affected by this disease. How could this happen? Because Susan and Nancy touched people on an emotional and spiritual level, and they have ignited the passion and fire that dwells in the heart.

> At its center, inspiration comes from touching people at their emotional/spiritual core.

Inspiration moves people to action. Action leads to increased energy and excitement. You can't buy inspiration; it must be created. Inspiration is created by individuals for individuals.

Chapter 12:
Vision and Developing Others

"A leader is one who knows the way, goes the way, and shows the way."

John C. Maxwell

Vision

Leaders must possess the ability to create vision for their followers and organization. It puzzles me how many leaders with whom I speak; explain their organization's vision as "we are just trying to keep our head above water." Really? That's your vision, to keep your head above water? With that as a vision, the organization will be lucky to manage that feat. Great leaders use their vision to inspire others. What type of inspiration does keeping your head above water create?

Before 1980 Americans received the news from newspapers, radio or from one of the three major television networks ABC, CBS, and NBC. These newscasts were primarily broadcast for a few hours in the early evening. Ted Turner, a broadcaster in the Atlanta, Georgia, market, had a vision of a twenty-four-hour news network. Most scoffed at the idea. But Turner continued to share his vision and even announced a deadline of being on the air in one year. That seemed like an impossible feat to most. Even though the project was undercapitalized, Turner held true to his

> Great leaders regardless of what is going on around them, have visions that take them beyond today and propel them into tomorrow.

vision. A former country-club building was used as the headquarters. The critics had said the project would fail in its first year. On June 1, 1980 CNN (Cable News Network) went on the air. Since then it has revolutionized the way Americans and the world receive news. To some degree it has changed the culture all together. Our whole expectation of news has changed. We expect to see live coverage while the event is happening. Truly that was the genius of Ted Turner's vision. But it would have been impossible for him to achieve this vision alone. It took more than one man to make this vision a reality. It took individuals coming together as a team with a purpose to turn the vision into a reality.

Don Soderquist, former CEO of Wal-Mart, describes a meeting that occurred in 1971 with Sam Walton and other executives of eight small regional discount stores in his book "The Wal-Mart Way".(1) At that time Wal-Mart was the thirty-sixth largest discount chain in America. The larger retailers had sales in the billions—Sears had sales of 9.3 billion, JC Penney at 4.2 billion, and K-Mart was at 2.5 billion. As part of this meeting, the executives went around the room and shared where they thought their sales would be in ten years. One CEO said their current sales were 40 million, and he believed they could reach 80 million. The next was at 80 million and said they would be at 100 million, and yet one more was currently at 100 million and projected to reach 160 million. Mr. Walton stated his sales were 44 million, and he expected to reach two billion! Ten years later Wal-Mart, through the vision and high expectations of Sam Walton, exceeded two billion. Today Wal-Mart is the largest company in the world and employees 2,100,000 worldwide and in 2010 net sales topped 405 billion.(2) (3)

Without vision neither Sam Walton nor Ted Turner would have been as successful. Vision is a leadership fundamental. It's important to understand that vision functions on more than one level. It touches people in multiple ways, and it produces results that cannot be duplicated by any other method.

Listed here are a few of the benefits of vision:

- Inspires

- Provides direction

- Sets priorities

- Energizes a team

- Keeps focus

- Helps others find their purpose

- Empowers

- Provides hope

- Encourages

The great leaders have a vision. They have a method for sharing that vision and the goal-reaching program to fulfill that vision. With vision fulfillment comes new visions, more confidence, and the ability to attract other leaders and followers. Vision filling is a rewarding moment for all involved.

Recruiting/Attracting

To accomplish your leadership goals, you must build and develop a team. One person has limits; a leader who attracts followers has fewer limits, and the leader who attracts other leaders has no limits. Regardless of the type of industry you are in, attracting others is essential for growth. If you are a church leader, you may call it conversions or new members. If you lead a sales team, you need to attract new sales staff and new clients. Whatever the case, it comes down to attracting and recruiting.

Where?

Everywhere you go you are potentially contacting an important part of your team. This is why you should always be aware of the impression that you are making and the picture you are painting.

Diversity

Often I find that leaders look to attract people who are similar to them. I understand the practice; we all want to be around people who share our habits. However as you build your team, the key is to attract others that share your purpose and passion but are diverse. A diverse team is a strong team.

Presenting an Opportunity

To present an opportunity, you first must know what the opportunity is and then you must believe in it. Having built multiple successful teams, I have found that you must be willing to share your opportunity with passion and conviction. Being fully aware that the right opportunity for one person may not be the right opportunity for another person. Each time you present an opportunity or share your vision it deepens your own resolve and belief in it. Presenting the opportunity is as much about you as it is about them. The point is, you must share the opportunity and vision if you want to grow your team with talent rich and purposed people.

Training or Development

Is training and developing the same thing? Most leaders never give this is a thought, but the reality is they are different. True, some of the same elements are present for each, however the purpose is different. As my good friend Debbie Cunningham says, "You train animals, you develop people." I have come to find a lot of wisdom in that statement. Yet churches and large global organizations all have training programs. The basic goals of these programs are to show you how to complete a task to the required specifications. In most cases you could substitute training with the word programming. As leaders we need to seek more than to program people; we must develop people. There is tremendous power in educating and developing others. Rather than bringing people into a training facility, we need to bring them into our development facility. Consider for a moment the psychological difference you would have if you entered into a training program or a development program. Just the term development sets expectations higher and produces a higher sense of importance to the individual. I'm not suggesting that you simply

> As leaders we need to seek more than to program people, we must be developing people.

128

change the name of the program and your facility. I'm recommending you consider changing the focus from training to developing and in doing so, put into motion the elements that are required to fulfill the mission of developing. Shed the limited mindset of merely training for the much broader view of development.

Everyone involved in the program will undergo a mental shift. Each person will understand that the program will have taken on a much greater purpose. The key is the more development that occurs the more value is built. The greater the value, the greater the influence those involved will be willing to give. Remember managers are trainers. Leaders are developers.

Ways to Develop Others

I devoted a lot of time in this book to the thought of developing others as a key component of great leadership. The question is how do you develop people? There are countless ways and methods that you can use to begin the development. It would be wise if you begin to think about your particular environment and the resources available to you to create development opportunities. There will be different levels of development for the different levels of your followership. The core team that you assemble will have a different developmental strategy than others. However nearly any situation at anytime can be used as a developmental moment. Often we limit ourselves with the view that only preplanned events can be the development, I have found that those are good opportunities and are essential to the process, but it is the moments that just happen that tend to have the greatest impact.

Chapter 12: Vision and Developing Others

Here are ten simple ways to begin to develop others.

1.   Invest your time with them

2.   Share ideas and thoughts

3.   Include them on important meetings

4.   Encourage an ownership mentality

5.   Communicate

6.   Share your reasoning behind key decisions

7.   Delegate responsibility

8.   Increase their authority

9.   Create experiences

10.   Encourage their personal development

This is a mutually chosen team. You have chosen them, and they have chosen you. These are the people with whom you share purpose and they have given you the gift of influence. Together you and your team will experience great success, but you can't be concerned about holding back. Great leaders know the more they give, the more they will receive.

The Things Words Can't Teach

There are some things that you just can't teach with words. Your actions will be the lesson. For example, every few weeks I take flowers and a card home to my wife to let her know how important she is and how much I value her in my life. I make it a point to do this on a day that I pick up our children from school. We go to the store together, and we pick out the flowers and cards. As I've said before, I have three children under seven years old, and they have a hard time agreeing on anything. It certainly would be much easier and would take less time for me to do this without their help. Yet, I invest the time because I want them to understand the lesson words can't teach. For my daughter, I want her to learn that she can expect to be treated with respect and that she has value. For my sons, the lesson is to value women and to treat them with a high level of respect and appreciation. How much more powerful is the lesson that they are learning by having them involved in the process? The same is true in our professional leadership; there are lessons we just can't teach by talking. Words will not substitute for involvement. We must teach these lessons by doing and by having those we seek to develop engaged in the process. This is a major portion of the development of our followers. As leaders, we need to be constantly seeking these types of opportunities to develop others through these experiences.

Coaching/Counseling Others

My mentor and friend Tracy Plaisance has always said, "You're not doing anybody any favors by not telling them the truth as it pertains to their performance. If you care enough to try not to hurt their feelings, then you should care enough to be honest and tell them the truth, so they can improve and be the best they can be." There is a line that leaders walk to encourage and not discourage, however the other side of the coin is that we need to develop people; it would be impossible to develop others without discussing areas where improvement is needed. The key is in the way we do it. Often we have developed a personal relationship with those in our core group and fear of damaging the relationship prevents us from making decisions or having conversations we need to have. As leaders we cannot afford to allow this to happen. If you are leading them, then you have the responsibility to bring to their attention areas that can be improved to make them stronger. Part of developing into a leader with lifelong influence is having these types of conversations. It should be viewed as a growth opportunity for all involved. Here are some techniques to maximize your coaching sessions.

1. **Never belittle or degrade**

This is an opportunity for growth. Growth comes from nurturing not tearing down.

2.   **Always in private**

Praise in public and council in private. No one likes to be embarrassed or humiliated. If you humiliate, you will certainly have lost anything positive that could have been gained by the opportunity.

3.   **Get to the point**

Don't beat around the bush, get to the point. Beating around the bush is a sign of not being confident and shows that you are unsure. Get to the point; do not make small talk or waste time. You are there for a specific reason—address it.

4.   **State the issue/problem/situation**

The issue must be clearly stated and brought out into the open. Stay on topic and don't wander into unrelated areas.

5.   **Ask questions**

It's imperative that you understand all the facts associated with the issue. By asking open-ended questions you will be able to get the information to which you otherwise didn't have access. Seek to understand an explanation but never accept an excuse.

6.   **Be clear about the resolution**

All parties must be clear on how the issue will be resolved and the steps to be taken. If it's appropriate, offer help; you should always attempt to leave the session with a clear resolution.

7.   **Share with them your vision for them**

Sharing your vision for them helps affirm the value that you have in their ability. It provides them with the feeling of hope and security.

8.   **End the session with something positive**

You will always want to end the session with something positive and motivational. Chances are they will reflect on the meeting and leaving with a positive tone will serve to energize rather than demoralize.

9.   **It's not who's right but what's important**

It's not about being right; it's about what is important. When we keep that in focus we tend to cut out the personal feelings that prevent us from moving forward.

10.   **View this as an opportunity**

This is an opportunity for all involved to develop to reach past their potential. Keep this in perspective as you navigate the session. Use the time and maximize the opportunity.

Know that as a leader, you will coach/council others; it is part of the development process. Don't hide from them, embrace the opportunity that they provide.

Pareto Principle 80/20

The principle began in 1895 when Italian economist, Vilfredo Pareto observed that 80 percent of Italy's land was owned by 20 percent of the population. This caused people to begin to analyze other aspects of life. The more they looked the more they discovered the 80/20 ratio seemed to apply to everything. Today the 80/20 Rule is the accepted business philosophy. In essence the rule states that the relationship between the input and output is rarely, if ever balanced. Here is how it looks.

- 80 percent of your time will be invested in 20 percent of the people.

- 80 percent of staff issues are created by 20 percent of the staff.

- 20 percent of your staff produces 80 percent of your results.

- 20 percent of your daily activities out produce the other 80 percent.

Remember the 80/20 Rule is only a guideline. It could be 70/30 or 85/15 the point is a small amount of something is responsible for the majority of results. By knowing this principle, you will be able to analyze your team exploring the most successful elements to properly allocate resources to the proper areas.

Planning for a Successor

All things have a beginning and an end. It's the way nature works. So why would we, as leaders think we could circumvent nature? Why wouldn't we plan for this? Part of any great leader's strategy is planning for your successor. Yet everyday businesses and organizations of all sizes struggle and some eventually fail because their leaders did not prepare the organization for this event. This is a costly mistake we cannot afford to make. However great leaders are always developing others, and it's this development that prepares the way for a leadership transition. This is a principle that is difficult to embrace for the underdeveloped leader. They view developing someone or a group of people who will eventually succeed them as foolish and dangerous. These viewpoints are for the small and narrow minded, and are born of the fear of being replaced unwillingly. The reality is great leaders are not replaced; they leave a mark that continues. Great leaders may repurpose their lives and move to other challenges but rarely are great leaders replaced by an organization. In the event that it did happen, you will have gained more by developing others than you would have ever lost.

Identifying a Successor

It is difficult to have a succession plan if you are not attracting and developing leaders. First the fundamental principles must be followed, so that we will be able to build a strong leadership base. Here is a technique to assist you in identifying your core leadership team. Knowing fully that 20 percent of your following will be producing 80 percent of the results. The first step is to look within that 20 percent to find your core leaders. When we apply the Pareto Principle to the remaining 20 percent we will be left with a good place to search for your core leadership team. These are the individuals you should invest 80 percent of your time with.

> Nothing great is ever accomplished without discipline and sacrifices.

Discipline and the Large Picture

Since the beginning of time, mankind has struggled with self-discipline. For those who master it, the world is an open door. We have created a culture of fast food and instant gratification. This has served to compound the lack of self discipline problem. However for the leader that remains disciplined opportunities will be abundant. You must condition yourself to sacrifice today's gratification for the treasures of tomorrow. This is true in every aspect of your life. You cannot lose weight and become physically healthy by eating high-fat junk food and refusing to exercise. It's only the disciplined person who delays the gratification, and eats healthy food and sacrifices time and comfort to exercise who will ever lose weight and become healthy. The same is true of the leader who must always be aware of the larger picture as it relates to the team and the organization. We see this played out every day with companies whose appetite for growth causes it to take unnecessary debt and risks. Later they find the growth was not sustainable because the proper steps were not taken to ensure a firm platform. Pat Parelli says, "Take the time it takes and it will take less time." How many times have we seen others rush projects only to have it fall apart and have to do it over again. If only they would have taken the time it took to do it right it would have taken less time. As leaders we need to be disciplined and take the time it takes holding to the solid foundations that serve the larger picture.

Chapter 13:
P.H.D. Goal Reaching System

"Picture yourself in your mind's eye as having already achieved this goal. See yourself doing the things you'll be doing when you've reached your goal."

Earl Nightingale

Goal-Reaching System

G oals are to a great leader as essential as oxygen is to the world. It's impossible to survive without them. Earl Nightingale once said, "People with goals succeed because they know where they're going." Goals are the roadmap to your destination. Think about this scenario: you and 999 other people are in a remote area in Wyoming. I asked each of you to come to my home, and when you get there, I will have the keys to a wonderful, wealth-filled life. You would probably be pretty excited about that. Here is the catch: I don't give you the state that I live in or my address. You will be traveling alone and without a map, GPS, or any other navigational device. Any road signs you encounter would be written in a language that you don't understand. The only thing you are given is a vehicle and one tank of gas. How excited are you now? Where would you start? How would you prepare? How long would you drive before you settled for someone else's home, even though you knew what you really wanted was somewhere else, just waiting for you to arrive? How many out of the 1,000 people would ever reach my home and get the keys to the life of their dreams? Obviously, we will never know, but this happens every day to people who live their

> "If you go to work on your goals, your goals will go to work on you. If you go to work on your plan, your plan will go to work on you. Whatever good things we build end up building us."
>
> -Jim Rohn

life without goals. They may have some vague idea of how they wish they could live, but it's just a wish. It's the same thing with our leadership. We must set a clear path for our team and ourselves. It's imperative that we have clear goals, clear roadmaps, and clear direction in our personal and professional lives. Can you imagine giving the above outlined task to your team? Of course not, but we do that daily by not having a goal-reaching program in place.

Through my research and my personal life, I believe that the majority of individuals have either no idea or the wrong ideas about goals. Often times we will hear about goal setting and its importance from life coaches, professional speakers, or perhaps a business associate. But notice the words they all use is *goal setting*. I believe that those words themselves are conveying the wrong message. That message that is being sent to our mind can become problematic. I would encourage you to strike the words goal setting from your vocabulary and thoughts and replace it with the idea of goal reaching. Setting goals is the easy part. We need to focus on reaching the goals if we are to ever reach past our potential.

I have spent more than twenty-five years studying and applying the best practice that I have learned about goals. I have compiled all that I have learned into the P.H.D. Goal Reaching System that is outlined here. This system has proven to be powerful and effective. This system, if followed, is guaranteed to bring you personal success in all areas of your life. There has not been a great leader that didn't have some type of goal system in place. It's merely not enough to write it, as is the case in most goal setting programs. The P.H.D. Goal Reaching System is founded on action. It's about high-yield, measurable action and accelerating the speed with which your goals are reached. The system outlined here is comprised of five stages, and each stage builds on the other.

Stage One

*   *Identify the Goal*

The goal must be realistic and specific. It must also be identifiable as well as measurable.

Stage Two

*   *List the Costs*

What will you have to sacrifice to reach the goal? There will always be a sacrifice to make. Some of the most common are time, energy, comfort, sleep, and money and/or relationships. Ask yourself if you are prepared to make the sacrifices necessary to reach the goal?

Stage Three

*   *Writing the Goal*

Once we write the goal, it starts to become reality. Up until this point, it is just a thought. But once we write it down, we begin to program the mind to look for opportunities to achieve it. Here are the most effective ways to write the goals to open the subconscious mind.

1.   Must be personal

2.   Must be written in the present tense

3.   Must be specific

4.   Must be positive

5.   Must be empowering

6.   Must include a deadline

Here is an example of how a typical goal might be written:

I need to make more money.

The way that this goal is written, it fails to connect. It does not include the present tense, positive, empowering, or the deadline elements of proper goal writing. Remember it's more than just putting it on paper; it's about properly programming your mind. Look at how much more powerful this goal becomes when all six elements are included.

I earn $8,000 a month because I work hard and bring value to my company by January 1.

Here are the specific elements of the statement broken down.

I earn (personal/present tense) *$8,000 a month* (specific) *because I work hard and bring value to my company* (positive/empowering) *by January 1.* (deadline)

Here is another example:

I lead my team with integrity and develop each member, and that increases our sales 1 million dollars by July 14.

I lead my team (personal/present tense) *with integrity and develop each member,* (positive/empowering) *and that increases our sales 1million dollars* (specific) *by July 14.* (deadline)

Stage Four

- *Action Plan*

If you only did the first three stages, you would be more successful than most in reaching your goals. Largely because of the incredible power that the subconscious mind has when programmed properly. Stage Four, the action plan, gives us the steps that we have developed to reach our goals. It is the roadmap that we will use. It's important to understand that even the best plans will have to be revised as you go. It is impossible to know every twist and turn that will be encountered on the way to reaching the goal. The important thing is that we will be engaged every step of the way. In my opinion one of the most vital parts to the process is knowing the first steps to take and then taking them. Creating momentum takes more effort and energy than maintaining momentum. The action plan is designed to help create the momentum and keep it going.

The larger the goal, the more detailed the action plan needs to be. There are some goals that may not require an extensive action plan, but all goals need to be accompanied by an action plan regardless of the size. The action plan will vary depending on if it is a team goal or personal goal.

A typical action plan will:

1.   Break the goal down into smaller goals.

2.   Details the steps necessary to reach the goal.

3.   List the resources needed, i.e., human, financial, personal, physical/structural, and material.

4.   Include an element to measure progress.

5.   Provide a detailed time line.

Stage Five

•   *Daily Reaching*

Daily reaching is intended to keep the goal real and alive. So often we get busy with other things and let life sidetrack our plans. The action plan may call for periods where progress is slow and unexciting. The key is to not lose sight of our goal and keep programming our minds to look for the opportunities. Daily reaching is designed to keep us motivated and feeling the emotions of how life will be when we reach the goal.

1.   Write the goal at least once in the morning and once throughout the day ideally close to bedtime. Write the goal in the format as described in stage three. The more you write the goal, the deeper the impression you make on your subconscious. You should always physically write the goal; do not use a computer to type it. It becomes more personal and powerful when it is actually written on a sheet of paper.

2.   Spend at least one minute three times a day visualizing the way you will feel when you reach the goal.

The more time you spend in positive thought about the goals, the more powerful the desire for those goals will become. As the desire increases, so will your action. The goal-reaching program is about action. Without action, you merely have wishes not goals. As Thomas Jefferson said, "Nothing can stop the man with the right mental attitude from achieving his goal; nothing on earth can help the man with the wrong mental attitude."

Chapter 14:
Time Management

"Lost time is never found again."

Benjamin Franklin

Time Management

We have all experienced the effects of a phenomenon known as Parkinson's Law. Parkinson's Law states…

Work expands to fill the time allotted for it.

If we don't establish firm deadlines for ourselves and others, then we will continue to expand the work and put it off. Great leaders realize that they must be able to counter Parkinson's Law to be effective. The greatest counter strategy is a good time management program.

> The first step of being able to leverage time is to value time.

Time is the one thing that just doesn't care about who you are or where you've been. Time doesn't discriminate between the rich or poor, young or old. There are twenty-four hours in a day and sixty minutes in an hour. We all have the same access to time; therefore we have the same opportunity to leverage it. What separates successful people from others is what they do with their time: how they manage it and more importantly how they invest it. Time is a valuable resource, and without it nothing else seems to matter. The key is for us to leverage our time, so we can maximize the harvest from it.

I suspect that those of us who are blessed to live a long life will someday understand how precious time really is. However generally at that stage of our lives, we have wasted more time than we have left.

Here are three guidelines to consider.

- The first step of being able to leverage time is to value time

- We must invest the majority of our time in activities that produce high-end results

- The remainder can be invested on activities with lesser results

There are some who take a narrow-minded view and equate high-end results to mean only income-producing results. High-end results should include income-producing activities, but it's much larger than that. It encompasses family time, time for yourself, spiritual time, and any other activities that you personally view as a high-end result.

The program that I currently use and teach is a combination from a number of systems that I have learned through the years. I have found if the system itself is time consuming, then it defeats the point. I purposely streamlined this program and kept it as simple as possible. The most important thing to know is whatever system you use will be more effective than not using any system at all.

The tasks are broken down into one of four categories.

1. ***Have to Do***

- These are tasks that produce high-end results.
- They have serious repercussions if not completed.
- These activities have firm deadlines.

2.   *Need to Do*

- These are tasks that you need to accomplish.
- They have a moderate end result.
- They have some repercussions if not completed.
- They should have deadlines.

3.   *Might Do*

- These are tasks that you would accomplish if time permits.
- They have low-end results.
- They have no repercussions if not completed.
- They wouldn't have deadlines.

4.   *Could Delegate*

- These are tasks that you could delegate to another.
- They could vary from high, medium, and low-end results.
- They could carry repercussions if not completed.
- If delegated, they will always have a deadline.

Under each category you will prioritize each task/project by three elements.

- **Deadline:**

When does it need to complete.

- **Degree of return:**

Is this a high return or low return task/project?

- **Importance:**

Are other team members waiting for this to complete their portion of the project?

Assigning a letter A-Z to that task/project under one of the four categories, begin with A and finish that task/project before moving onto B. Never work on a *Need to Do* task/project if you have something in the *Have to Do* category. Eliminate all unnecessary bouncing back and forth from task to task while completing only a portion at a time. The practice of task hopping generally steals time from you. The point is to invest the majority of time in the activities that produce high-end results. The balancing act is not to invest more time than necessary with each project; remember, we are attempting to counter Parkinson's Law.

Delegation

One of the best lessons you will learn is to effectively delegate. I personally struggled with this for years. I bought into the old saying, If you want something done right, do it yourself. I felt so strong about it that I, with the help of my dad and father-in-law, built the house where my family lives. The fact that I struggled with delegation is perhaps an understatement. When I became serious about changing my life, I found that I wasn't so concerned about getting things done "right." That was the lie I told myself, the truth was I wanted to be in total control. When I began to repurpose my life, I knew it was time to deal with the control issues that had not only affected my leadership but also my personal relationships. I share this with you so that you can be aware that if you struggle with delegation, it's very possible that the core issue is control and delegation is the side issue. When you set aside your control issues, you will begin to see clearly how proper delegation can become a powerful tool in both the development of your team as well as yourself.

Delegation Classification

I want to introduce you to a simple two-part rating system based on the importance level of the project and the skill set necessary to complete the project. Here is how the system works. Every project will be rated based on two categories, the Importance Level and the Skill Level it will take to

"No person will make a great business who wants to do it all himself or get all the credit."

-Andrew Carnegie

complete the project. Each category is based on a 10 point rating system. The numbers 1,2,3 are considered low 4,5,6,7 are considered medium and 8,9,10 are the highest rating.

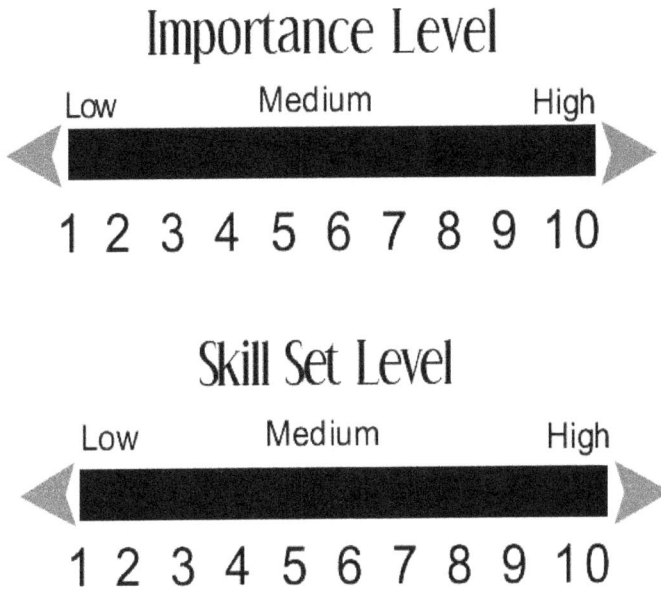

Importance Level

Low　　　　Medium　　　　High

1 2 3 4 5 6 7 8 9 10

Skill Set Level

Low　　　　Medium　　　　High

1 2 3 4 5 6 7 8 9 10

(Diagram 14.1)

By identifying these two basic elements, you will be able to assign the project to the right person or team of people. This is particularly beneficial when you use delegation as a development tool. For example you might have a low importance level but a medium skill set level. This would be an ideal situation to develop a person who is not yet at a medium skill level but can be given the opportunity to help reach that level.

It is important to keep in mind that you might be the only one who understands the classification of the project from the organizations perspective. If you do a proper job in matching the skill set level, individuals will be operating at their personal high level. Your followers will classify the project as a high importance level and high skill set level based upon the fact that they are operating at their personal high skill set level. That, in and of itself, creates a high level of importance to the person. It must always be viewed from the follower's perspective. Great leaders understand how important it is to use this opportunity to build value. Don't ever underestimate the power of even a low importance level and low skill set level project can have on a person. Use this opportunity to build and develop the members of your team.

Delegation as a Tool

Delegation is a necessary process in becoming a great leader. Delegation provides numerous benefits to the parties involved. Depending on the type of project that is being delegated, delegation can be a tremendous asset. Here is a list of some of the common purposes proper delegation can serve:

1.   Time management tool

2.   Development of individual team members/followers

3.   Conveys your confidence in them

4.	Builds trust

5.	Creates motivation

6.	Helps creating ownership

7.	Promotes teamwork

8.	Used as a reward (should not be used as punishment)

9.	Efficient

10.	Can create healthy competition

Delegation, when used correctly can be one of the best friends to leaders. Because we all have a need to feel important, to be recognized, and to contribute, this is a great area on which to focus. Delegation is a great tool to help develop people. In many cases delegation can be viewed as an opportunity. Opportunity tends to carry a level of responsibility, which conveys your confidence in them. Confidence in them produces pride, trust, and ownership. Ownership gives way to motivation. Motivation can ignite a person to achieve greatness.

How to Delegate

Ronald Reagan, the fortieth president of the United States, is reported to have said, "Surround yourself with the best people you can find, delegate authority, and don't interfere." Here are seven ideas to assist in the delegation process.

1.   Identify how many people are needed to complete the project.

2.   Assign the lead responsibility.

3.   Give a clear vision of what you want.

4.   Set the expectations.

5.   Give a deadline.

6.   Let them figure out the steps to completing the project.

7.   Don't manage the project—just the end result

A key point to delegation is that it should never be used to push your work off on others. If it becomes viewed as your way to push off work by your team, you will have created a major leadership issue and rendered a powerful tool useless.

The temptation for most leaders is to delegate but not give away the control. Once you have delegated the project, it is imperative to allow the project lead the freedom to lead the project. Let them have the full benefit of the experience.

"The best executive is the one who has sense enough to pick good men to do what he wants done, and self-restraint enough to keep from meddling with them while they do it."

-Theodore Roosevelt

"Never tell people how to do things. Tell them what to do, and they will surprise you with their ingenuity."

-George S. Patton

Chapter 15:
The YOU Factor

"Be a yardstick of quality. Some people aren't used to an environment where excellence is expected."

Steve Jobs

What's in a Name

As leaders, we must always be aware that our name speaks volumes about us. Our name precedes us most of the time. People hear our name and have preconceived notions about us long before they meet us. In our lifetime we will possess many things. Some will be very valuable, and others will not. Consider the value of your name. Regardless of where you have come from, you have the ability to add value in every way to your name. It is one of the greatest tools you have, and so often we discount it as meaningless. I believe your name is one of the most important things you posses.

Name Brand

Companies spend millions of dollars every year on name recognition; companies do not just want us to remember their name—they want us to connect it with a particular thought or emotion. Why? Because they understand the power that names can posses, and you too can use the same principles to develop your "name brand," and it won't cost millions.

Everyone lives within their own microcosm. This is your market; it's made up of people, places, and events. You live, work, and play in your market. By leveraging your actions, you can effectively build your "name brand" within a short amount of time. In fact, you have already been doing it. Even though you may have never given thought to what you want people to connect your name with, it is human nature to affix labels and emotions subconsciously to people, places, and things. Knowing this we can help create the feeling, thoughts, and emotions that generate positive reactions.

Perhaps one of the best examples that I have ever witnessed is that of Jeff Mingledorff, who by all accounts has established strong name recognition in his community. Jeff has served in the United States Marine Corps for over twenty-five years. He is an Iraq War veteran and has risen to the ranks of sergeant major. Anyone who has had contact with Sergeant Major Mingledorff knows exactly who he is and what he stands for. He is active in the community and always looks for ways to serve. He has dedicated his life to the purpose of the United States Marine Corps. He is a dynamic speaker and delivers his presentations with the passion and precision of a marine. If you have ever had contact with him, when you think of a marine, you will think of Sergeant Major Mingledorff. He has built his name brand based on his actions, convictions, and strong leadership example. You too can do the same. Here are some action steps that you can take to begin to develop and leverage your name brand.

1.   **Indentify your message**

- What do you want to convey to people?

- What do you want others to associate you with?

- What thoughts or emotions do you want others to feel about you?

- What do you want others to remember about you?

2.   **Your name goes where you go and some place you don't**

- Your actions, behavior and words must be consistent with the message. They cannot conflict.

- Others will carry your name to places and people you will never go or people you may never meet.

3.   **Do what you say/ hold yourself accountable**

- Make commitments and then follow through on them.

- Nothing will hurt you faster than not following up on your word.

- Don't make excuses.

4.   **Actions speak louder than words**

- Let your actions be evidence of your message.

- Let others bring attention to your actions.

5.   **Be humble**

•   Regardless of your message, humility must be part of it.

I was told of a story about a well known minister who was very influential with his followers and others. He spoke to millions of people throughout his ministry. He counseled presidents and other powerful people of the day. His name was synonymous with serving and preaching the gospel of Christ. He understood the power of his name brand and protected it at great cost. He never wanted to damage the brand that he had built or compromise the gift of influence that he had received from others. He understood that any appearance of impropriety would limit his ability to share his purpose with others. I'm told that for this very reason if he was riding in an elevator alone and someone from the opposite sex entered, he would kindly step off and wait for the next elevator. What a tremendous amount of conviction it took to put such a practice in place. He knew that just an appearance of wrongdoing could create a situation that could damage the brand and limit his ability to fulfill his purpose.

You are building your name brand with each word you speak, with each step you take, and even with each thought you think. What do you want your brand to be known for? When your name is mentioned what do you want people to think of? It's shocking just how many people overlook the value of their name. Take for instance the late JFK Jr. He was obviously very well connected and operated in the circle of high society. It's reported that JFK Jr. made $25,000 to introduce people to someone they really wanted to meet. JFK Jr. understood the value of his name. The value I want you to focus on is not the monetary value, but the value that generates influence and paves the way to the influence endorsement and leverages the influence echo effect.

We will work our entire life to build our name brand, but we can destroy it in seconds with our actions. Your name is a great treasure that you possess and it never has to stop increasing in value. Guard it. Guard it from others, but more importantly guard it from yourself.

ATTITUDE

Attitude affects everything that we do. It is the way you mentally approach a person or situation. Your attitude sets a tone for how you interact with others and how others will interact with you. Attitude produces energy like an aura around you that others receive and interpret. In turn, attitude also affects your thoughts. The more positive your attitude, the more positive your thoughts will be. No one can read your thoughts, but everyone can read your attitude.

You have ultimate control over your attitude. You can allow circumstance or people to influence your attitude, but you have the ultimate control. With ultimate control comes ultimate responsibility to keep it positive.

Years ago I was shown a simple way to demonstrate the importance of attitude. You take each letter in the word attitude and assign it with the number it holds in the place of the alphabet. When those numbers are added together it produces 100.

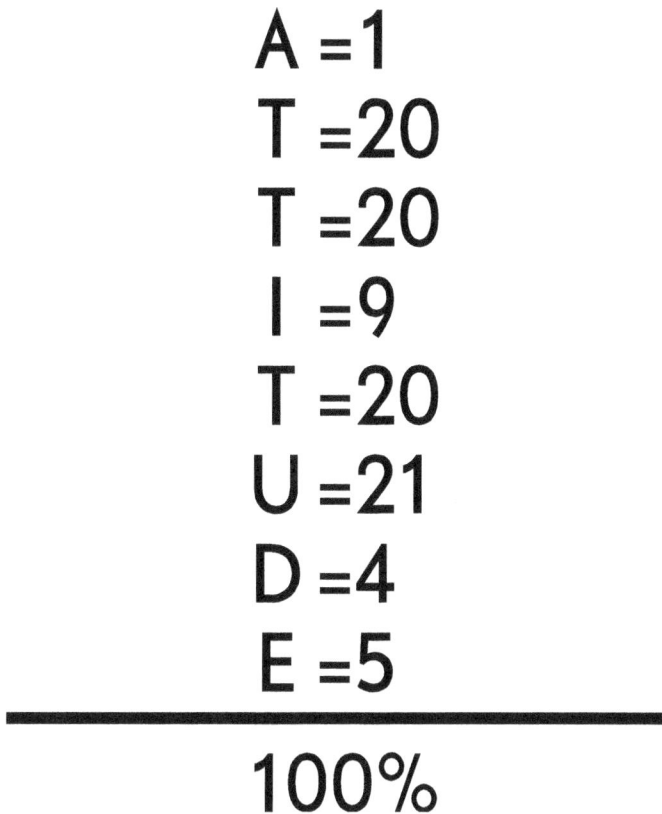

$$A = 1$$
$$T = 20$$
$$T = 20$$
$$I = 9$$
$$T = 20$$
$$U = 21$$
$$D = 4$$
$$E = 5$$
$$\overline{}$$
$$100\%$$

(Diagram 15.1)

The explanation was that your attitude matters 100 percent of the time. I like to take it one step further and say not only does it matter 100 percent of the time—you control it 100 percent of the time.

You choose to have a good attitude; you start by making that choice, and you support that choice with your thoughts and actions. Great leaders know the importance of attitude and how it affects the team. The leader's attitude sets the team's attitude. Recently I was speaking with a client and her team, and I asked her how things were going for them. Immediately her body posture slumped and her tone changed as she said, "We are barely hanging on." Her team's eyes were downcast and the mood changed instantly. They had adopted her attitude. I explained to her privately that financially they may have been barely hanging on, but other areas of the organization were thriving. She needed to concentrate on those areas when she felt defeated because of the affect her attitude was having on her team. The reality was that if she didn't change her attitude, she would defeat herself long before finances would.

Confidence

In the classic book "Think and Grow Rich" by Napoleon Hill, he describes the story of a great warrior who lived many years ago.(1) He was faced with a decision to ensure his success. The warrior was preparing to face a fierce enemy who outnumbered his own army. He loaded his soldiers onto ships and sailed far away to the enemy's shores. After the soldiers and supplies were offloaded, he ordered that all the ships were to be burned. With the burning ships behind him, he addressed his army. "We are about to engage in a battle, a battle that will be long and hard, but a battle where we will be victorious. You see the smoke from the ships behind me. That means we cannot leave this shore unless we win. We will win together or we will perish together." With that he led the charge, and they were victorious against a larger and stronger enemy! You notice that he didn't leave one ship for himself just in case. He burned all the ships. He was fully invested. His men knew that he was with them no matter what, and they would fight as one. What type of confidence did that build in his men? Was there any doubt who was going to be victorious? They had chosen to win. We as leaders must have confidence in our ability to lead. We must have

> *"A pessimist sees the difficulty in every opportunity; an optimist sees the opportunity in every difficulty."*
>
> -Winston Churchill

confidence in our team, and most importantly we must inspire the confidence of our team to believe in themselves. If you lead long enough, you will be faced with a leadership opportunity. Many times these opportunities will come in the form of a crisis. While others will only see the crisis, you will see an opportunity, an opportunity that you will be prepared to capitalize on. Preparedness comes from consistently working on your leadership. Burn your ships and become fully invested. It is in these moments that great leaders are built.

Pressure vs. Stress

Is there a difference? Yes. Stress is negative in nature and is destructive. A life filled with stress will be a short life. Stress is a result of not being prepared for the situation. It operates with fear to create more stress. Pressure however is neutral. Pressure is being prepared and results in the ability to look at situations as opportunities to excel. This comes from the confidence that being prepared creates. Leaders invest time developing themselves and their team so both are prepared. While others are feeling anxiety, worry, and stress, those who are prepared are feeling confidence and excitement knowing that they have been presented an opportunity to excel.

A Picture Is Worth a 1,000 Words

We have all heard the saying that a picture is worth a 1,000 words. In the context of leadership I want you to be the art. I want you to see yourself through the eyes of the observer. It's common knowledge that people are constantly making judgments based on what they are observing. These judgments are the basis for determining whether they tune you in or tune you out. Most experts believe first impressions are created within the first ten to fifteen seconds of contact with you. The two largest contributors to first impressions are appearance and communication. Appearance is more than just how you look, it's how you carry yourself. Do you stand up straight or do you slouch? Do you display confidence or do you project arrogance? Communication is the words and tone we use, and the body language we display. It's safe to say that everything we do is painting a picture. That picture is worth much more than a 1,000 words, and the consequence for painting the wrong picture can be devastating.

In what ways do we paint the picture? In essence we paint the picture by the way we live our lives. From the amount of time we invest with people and what we say and do in that time. Do we give the minimal amount of time necessary and act as if that is a burden? Or do we give our attention and leave them encouraged? The way we treat people always matters. What is your appearance? Are you well groomed and organized or are you disheveled and unprepared? What picture are you painting? When we begin to look at our actions through the eyes of others we might begin to see a different picture than what we thought we were painting.

People You Surround Yourself With

Throughout the years I have had various roles within the organizations that I have served. One role that I have always enjoyed is that of the educator/developer. I have always liked the sense of accomplishment in helping one reach their goals. I have helped develop individuals in many fields and in a variety of positions. It never ceases to amaze me how the successful individuals will be drawn to other successful people. While those who make excuses for their lack of success quickly find people who share their negative, excuse driven mentality to associate with.

A few years back I was developing a new agent in the delivery of our presentation and our value proposition. We had spent time both in the classroom and in the field. As part of the development process he was scheduled to go with me to observe the presentation in action. I began to notice that every time he would go with me something would go wrong. At first I dismissed it. The more he went with me the ratio of new clients to appointments began to drastically decrease. I was puzzled. I had my wife listen to my presentation to pick up on anything that I might have been saying that I could correct. It just so happens there were a few weeks in our program that he was not with me. During those weeks my ratios shot right back up. Was I doing something different? Had I changed my delivery? Were the others bad appointments? All these thoughts were circulating through my head.

What was it? I am purposed to be the best that I can be, and part of that process is to objectively look to see how I can improve. I refuse to look for excuses or shift the blame to someone else. Because of that, I really didn't think that much about my new agent in the equation of the problem. I searched my demeanor, body posture, and gestures with no clear answer.

The next few appointments that we went on I started to pay closer attention not only to my perspective client but my new agent's body language and posture. There was the issue. I noticed that he was not engaged! He didn't appear to be attentive, interested, or even concerned about the issue that I was trying to solve for our prospective client. Even though I was fully engaged and was working to provide a solution to the client's issues, the perspective client read far more into the little subtle body language cues of the new agent. The cues were telling them something completely different than what I was attempting to present.

In any process building confidence is essential for moving the relationship forward. The same is true with regard to our leadership development. The people we surround ourselves with need to be as engaged in the process as we are. We can't be on two different pages in the book and expect others not to notice. They will be forced to choose which page to read. It is very unwise for a leader to put themselves in that position. Even though I might have been doing the correct things to build confidence and ultimately to gain influence, I was carrying around a neon sign that was giving the opposite message. These are things we must be aware of. Great leaders surround themselves with great people, individuals who have bought into the vision and have a passion for the purpose.

I brought the situation to the attention of the new agent. I shared my observations and concerns. Even though I had invested a considerable amount of resources in him, it became clear he didn't have the same vision, and his buy-in to our process was low. I made the decision that he was toxic to our organization, and he would jeopardize the goals we were reaching for. He was let go immediately. I have never regretted that decision or experience. As leaders we must always strive to surround ourselves with those people who have a similar purpose and the desire to achieve greatness.

What Type of Leader Are You?

There are two types of leaders—leaders who attract followers and leaders who attract other leaders. John Maxwell in his book "Mentoring 101" describes the limits of those who attract followers as "People who attract and team up with only followers will never be able to do anything beyond what they can personally touch or supervise." He goes on to say this about those who attract and recruit other leaders "But people who attract leaders influence many other people through their interaction. Their team can be incredible."(2) Mr. Maxwell is absolutely right; leaders who attract followers will always be limited in what they will accomplish. However the leader who attracts other leaders has no limits.

Leaders who attract only followers have these limiting behaviors and beliefs.

•   Difficulty letting go of control

- Need to touch every aspect of the operation

- Feel threatened by other leaders

- Enjoy being the only expert

- Crave the ego stroke from having the answers

- Lack vision

- Take all the credit and none of the blame

- Do not self-develop

- Do not invest in others development

Leaders who attract other leaders display these behavior and beliefs.

- Have incredible passion

- Encourage others to take control

- Give credit

- Celebrate the growth in others

- Have vision

- Understand the power of having others leaders

- Encourage others to develop the answers

- Mentors others

- Always self-developing

- Invest heavily in others

A significant part of becoming a great leader lies in your ability to be comfortable and secure with yourself. Being a great leader requires you to be a great developer of people. To do that, you must be one who seeks to develop yourself. I have never met or heard about a truly great leader who only attracted followers. I want you to make the shift mentally today from viewing your success as a leader by the quality of followers you attract to the quality of leaders you develop.

The GAME!

It seems to me that many leaders are confused about their role. I want you to think of this as a football game. In the game you have spectators, players, fans, and coaches. As the leader, which is your role? Let's examine roles and their importance to the game.

Spectators: This is anybody and everybody who is not on your team. These are the people you come in contact with daily and with whom you build your name brand. These are your clients, potential future team members, and these people watch you and your team daily.

Players: This is your team. They are the ones that play the game. They execute the plays that are designed to bring victory. Without the team, you have no need for the rest of the organization.

Fans: They cheer for the team. They give verbal support and are excited when the team scores. These are your friends and family, and they play a role in supporting the team.

Coach: The coach sets the tone. The coach designs the plays and corrects the players when they aren't reaching past their potential. The coach encourages the players when they are in the close games. The coach takes the field with the team and doesn't leave until every second is off the clock. The coach is consistently looking for great players to recruit to make the team stronger. The coach gives the credit to the team; he celebrates in the victories and gives encouragement in defeat.

As leaders we need to take the role of the coach. You will always see the coach on the sidelines with the team. Yet too often leaders want to hide away in the office and never go where the game is really being played. They fail to recruit for new talent to make their team better, and the moment it looks like the game is lost, they run off the field when there is still time left on the clock. You must be there; you must play till the end regardless of the score. You set the tone. You determine the intensity; you feed the desire to succeed. You are the coach you lead your team.

Four Types of People You Encounter

As the preacher paced back and forth on the stage he said, "There are four types of people you encounter daily."

1.   People you don't notice.

2.   People you do notice.

3.   People you notice and interact with.

4.   People you remember.

He went on to make the point that we needed to be the type of people that others remember because of our faith. It's unclear to me if he had read about these four types of people or his own observations led him to this discovery. However it came to be, it challenged me in more than one aspect of my life.

 As leaders we need to be the type of people that not only are remembered for our integrity, generosity, and the other abilities and attributes we have discussed. Equally important, we must be the type of people who remember. Remembering the details about others is a powerful principle in creating influence. When you truly take a sincere interest in people and begin to invest your time, effort, vision, and attention in them, you will remember details about them because it will become important to you. Ironically it's those tiny details that make people feel important. This sense of importance leads to a feeling of being valued. When you value your followers, they will go to amazing levels to meet your expectations.

Wal-Mart Ten-Foot Rule

Sam Walton knew how to serve his customers. If you read anything about Sam Walton you will soon realize that he had an incredible passion for serving his customers. Mr. Walton learned early about the ten-foot rule and implemented it into his company. Mr. Walton encouraged his associates to take the pledge "I promise that whenever I come within ten feet of a customer, I will look him in the eye, greet him, and ask if I can help."

I like to use a modified version of Mr. Walton's ten-foot rule. The ten-foot rule for leaders is...

Whenever I come within ten feet of a person, I will look them in the eye, smile, and when able, speak an encouraging word.

As leaders we can make quantum leadership leaps by putting this simple rule into practice within our own lives. When you become a leader you are in the people business. All people are your clients; all people have the ability to assist you in reaching past your potential. In turn you have the ability to help others reach past their potential as well.

Importance of Work Ethic

I was in attendance at an event that Joe Montana the four-time Super Bowl winner and Hall of Fame Quarterback was speaking. Joe recounted the story of Hall of Fame receiver Jerry Rice when he first joined the San Francisco 49ers. Joe said in practice Jerry would run his route, he would throw Jerry the ball, and after catching the ball, Jerry would run the rest of the length of the field and score a touchdown. The normal protocol was to catch the ball and run ten to fifteen yards, turn around, and run the play again. Joe commented that at first they all thought Jerry was just trying to be the hotshot to impress the coaches. But as they watched Jerry and saw his incredible work ethic, all the receivers started to run the rest of the way and score the touchdown. It eventually became a competition. Joe went on to say that Jerry's work ethic made the whole team better. I believe that it is this type of preparedness and work ethic that goes a long way in determining your success. Just as Jerry's work ethic influenced and helped propel the San Francisco 49ers to greatness, your work ethic will do the same for the team you lead.

Chapter 16:
Putting It All Together

"If your actions inspire others to dream more, learn more, become more, you are a leader."

John Quincy Adams

Lasting Effects

L et's look at the definition of purpose one more time. "The reason for which something exists or is done, made, used; an intended or desired result; end; aim; goal." Now look at the definition of influence: "A power affecting a person, thing, or course of events, especially one that operates without any direct or apparent effort." If we were to combine the two and insert the words *I, me,* and *purpose* it would read like this *"The purpose for which I exist; giving me the power to affect a person, thing, or a course of events!"* This is the definition that I want you to apply to your personal life as well as in your leadership. It is nearly impossible to become a great leader without purpose. Purpose breeds passion in great leaders, and we know people are attracted to passion-filled leaders. This purpose, combined with passion, influence, and application of the principles outlined in this book, will help you develop into the great leader that you desire to be. It will help you become the person who reaches past their potential and helps others do the same. Ultimately great leader's help others better themselves by development and help them fulfill their purpose.

At the core of every person there is an inherent need to be wanted. There is a desire to help and there is a burning desire to succeed. It's through life that we build layer on layer over this core distorting it, and in many cases distorting the truth. We build these layers as a defense mechanism to our environment. Perhaps it's for protection or self-preservation and maybe it's because we were just taught that way. So many times the best in people never gets exposed. It just sits there buried underneath, slowly being smothered by yet another layer of fear. Then we encounter those people who expose their core to others.

They risk rejection. They brave their own personal fears, and they dare to become great. How exciting that can be. How empowering the feeling. Let your purpose cut away the layers that have built on you and your team.

Managers and Employees: The A Factor

Most organizations will have the need to fill the positions of both managers and employees. We always seek to fill those roles with the right type of people. Dan Green the founder and CEO of Hobby Lobby built his company from a $600.00 investment into a 1.4 billion dollar enterprise. In his book "More Than a Hobby" he explains that the quality managers he seeks are *A* managers because of their integrity and work ethic. He adds that when *A* managers hire, they tend to hire other *A* type people. But when *B* managers hire, they often hire *C* type people because they are intimidated and fearful that the *A* person might show them up. This results in a weakening of the organization. When the *A* person finds himself working under the supervision of a *B* manager, the *A* person becomes frustrated quickly with the lack of the quality the *B* manager finds acceptable and seeks to leave the organization. While the *B* and *C* people hang on year after year, spreading their mediocrity. He adds that finding and nurturing *A* type people is incredibly important.(1)

This is a great point to keep in sight as you seek to build a stronger organization. An aspect of your leadership is to provide the strongest organization that you can for your team. Having the right people in the right positions is part of this. Setting the bar with high expectations and holding all accountable is crucial.

Elitism Leading

There is a lot of elitism leading in corporate America today. In fact this type of leadership is prevalent in all industries. There is no room for this style of leadership if you're set on becoming a great leader. I believe it is impossible to take an elitist mentality to leadership and transform into a great leader. They are opposites and are bound to oppose one another. Great leaders have a servant mentality while elitist leaders have a to-be-served mentality. If you strive to develop into a great leader, you must be on guard to ensure this ideology doesn't make its way into your leadership or the culture that you establish. This type of leadership has an aristocratic air to which many people will not respond favorably to.

As we've discussed, leaders are in the people business and each person has his own set of priorities that motivate them. We know that there are universal priorities that exist in all of us. By understanding them and appealing to them we can affect higher levels of influence. With all things there are also universal actions that produce the opposite effect. There are behaviors a leader can display that are contrary to the leadership fundamentals that will cause your followers to decrease the amount of influence given. Through development and the application of the knowledge, you will minimize the risk of this happening to you.

I don't believe that leaders purposely set out to demotivate their followership and for the most part leaders don't intend to create an environment that doesn't value the team. But the intent is second to the result in this case. Here are twelve common traits that devalue your followership.

Not following through:

Do what you say you're going to do and do it in a timely way. You must follow through with your commitments; this speaks to your dependability. Your followers must know that you can be counted on.

Improper priorities:

When an issue or idea has been brought to you for consideration, it is a priority for that person. While the subject may not be a priority issue, the fact that a follower brought it to you makes it such. Your followership is always a top priority. Great leaders never lose sight of the priority of the people.

Failing to communicate clearly:

We must always be evaluating all levels of our communication. The majority of what we do hinges on the ability to clearly and properly communicate. Unclear communication accounts for a large portion of wasted resources and leads to a frustrated followership.

Penthouse problem:

It is very difficult to lead from the penthouse office. You must go where the people are. Isolating yourself accomplishes just that; you become isolated. Isolation will always affect your ability to lead.

Preferred parking:

There is no better way to tell your followership that you think that you are better than they are than having your name on the parking space closest to the door. Many high-ranking officials within an organization do this. I can think of very few things that fly in the face of servant leadership like the appearance of elitism. Perhaps you lead in an organization that fosters this culture; if you really want to see your team respond, don't participate in it. Refuse to use the privileges normally afforded. People will talk. It's just the kind of talk leaders seeking high influence want.

Impressions:

Our leadership needs to be setting the proper impressions. Too many times leaders think that they should display their success to the team, and they flaunt the fact that they are golfing while their team/followers are stuck doing the work. I would caution you to look at the impression and the message that you are conveying. Are you telling them that you value the job they are doing? Be aware of the impression you are giving. Always make sure that the impression is consistent with your message.

Blaming others:

Society seems to breed those who seek to blame everyone else for missteps. A leader is the first person to accept full blame. You are ultimately the person who is responsible, so step up and be present and take responsibility. No excuses.

Taking the credit:

Give the credit away; don't keep it because it doesn't belong to you. It's the team's victory. It always comes back to pay you dividends.

Devaluing the team:

Constant ridiculing devalues the team. Saying things like "I could have done a better job with my eyes closed" or "If I wanted it done like this, I would have called a bunch of kids" or anything along those lines. This type of behavior devalues the team. Often it starts as insulting jokes but takes on a life of its own. It is good to have humor; however the joke should never be at the expense of the team.

Not being on time:

Anytime you're late it shows a lack of respect for those who have been waiting for you. I have heard leaders claim that they are always seven to ten minutes late on purpose to show authority. This is a poor practice to have. Authority and lack of respect for others are not in the same family. Being prompt and organized at the agreed upon time is a sign of strength and respect.

Not giving your attention:

Few things convey to others as strong a message as not giving them your full attention. I have been told that the average decision maker for companies has a seven-to-ten-minute attention span. It alarms me to know that in that short amount of time most aren't even giving it their full attention. When you are with people give them your attention.

White-knuckle control:

We all have seen those who fear losing control, they hold on to it so tight that if it were an object their knuckles would turn white because they were gripping it so hard. This is induced by fear. As we develop we make the mental shift from trying to hold onto control to sharing and delegating because we realize that this brings more control and greater results.

Leading is more about giving than it will ever be about receiving. Giving encompasses more than the physical or monetary. It's giving of your time, your attention, your focus, your purpose, your passion, your knowledge, your trust, and so much more. Make the shift, look to give rather than looking for what you can get.

The Cost of Poor Leadership

In the book "The Exceptional Presenter" Timothy J. Koegel states that according to the Association of Fraud Examiners, American business lose nearly 700 billion dollars of annual revenue to internal fraud every year. This accounts for nearly 5 percent of their annual revenue.(2) He contrasts that with the thought that poor presentations could account for that much or more in lost revenue. Yet the average business seems unconcerned with preparing presenters. While no data exists on how much poor leadership costs, we could all agree that it would be much more than 5 percent. And yet everyday many dismiss the idea of investing in developing leaders.

There is no way of knowing what could have been if only the proper leader had been in place. What are the costs to our children, when we don't have great leaders in education or our churches, local business, and our government? How many lives could have been positively influenced by great leadership? How many more opportunities could have been created? How much of an impact could an organization have on the world? This is

> The fact is poor leadership costs in every category, from revenue and opportunity, to purpose and fulfillment.

one of the reasons why it is so important to develop yourself and others. It is too costly to ignore; making the investment in leadership is a wise choice.

Ten Fundamental Leadership Pillars

Tens of thousands of books have been written on the subject of leadership, all trying to explain the art. Opinions vary, but all agree there is no magical formula. However there are principles and many examples of great leaders throughout history ready for examination. I have often been asked if I could condense leadership into ten specific points what would they be? I hesitate to answer such a question because it seems only to advance the idea of a quick-and-easy, one-size-fits-all fix for leadership, which I have found no evidence of such in existence. If I could only pass along ten points, they would be what I have classified as the ten fundamentals pillars of leadership:

Chapter 16: Putting It All Together

1.	Core Character

2.	Understanding and Living a P.H.D. Life

3.	Self-Development

4.	Being a Master Communicator

5.	The Ability to Inspire

6.	Visionary

7.	Establishing a Goal Reaching Plan

8.	The Ability to Attract Leaders and Develop People

9.	Establishing a Succession Plan

10.	Having a Servant Attitude

I believe that these are the ten fundamental pillars of building a great leader. By mastering and living these ten principles, you will establish an influence that is rarely seen. It will enable you to inspire people to reach past their potential while enabling you to do the same. The wisdom contained in these ten principles has the power to change the world. If I had to choose just one principle, it would be to develop a servant attitude. There are few things that develop the character and establish lasting influence as becoming a servant of mankind. There are countless people who have done just that, but I will list three here for your consideration: Jesus, Gandhi, and Mother Teresa. In the words of Jesus, as recorded in Matthew 23:11, "The greatest among you will be your servant." Over 2,000 years later there have never been truer words spoken.

Closing Thoughts

I want to leave you with sixteen of the most important points of this book. These points are crucial as you move forward in your leadership journey. I've come to embrace the fact that each of us is unique and bring our own perspectives to the conversation. It is my desire to have contributed to the discussion and have been able to provide you with some thoughts, ideas, and strategies that will accelerate you to reaching past your potential, catapulting you deeper into the process of developing into a great leader.

- You are in the people business.

- Have a strong clear vision.

- There are differences between a manager and a leader.

- Lead with a servant attitude, NOT a to-be-served attitude.

- Influence is vital to leadership.

- Integrity matters.

- Learn to communicate.

- Protect your name brand.

- Invest in the development of people.

- Goal reaching is different than goal setting.

- Purpose affects the heart, and reason affects the mind.

- Use flexible power.

- Inspire others.

- Ten Fundamental Pillars of Leadership.

- P.H.D. is the powerful key.

- Self-development is a must.

Sharing your purpose with others and living in a way that supports the fundamental principles outlined in this book will help people give you the gift of influence. This influence joined with your visions will create a force that will be undeniable.

Leadership is a lifelong journey, and it needs to be treated as such. Great leaders are not developed in a matter of months, but rather through years of experience and self-development. It is impossible for you to make progress and excuses at the same time. They are opposites, you must choose which path you will walk.

My hope for you is that you will aspire to reach past your potential in all aspects of your life. Fully knowing and believing that you are capable of achieving greatness and that you, and only you, are in control of your life. Understanding your mind holds the key that unlocks the door of your potential; it is your determination to see your purpose fulfilled that keeps you pressing forward; it's the quest to live a healthy and balanced life that brings the wonderful convergence of the P.H.D. leadership philosophy. It is purpose, health, and determination working together like a precision instrument seeking the opportunities to allow you to reach past your potential and ultimately resulting in achieving new levels of success.

My desire for you is to live and lead a purposed, healthy, and determined life, reaching past your potential in all areas.

Let's connect,

-Justin

For a special message from Justin scan this code.

Free Bonus Videos are available at

www.ThePHDLeader.com

Notes

Chapter 2

(1) Collins English Dictionary,10th edition Dictionary.com, accessed 8/01/2010,
http://dictionary.reference.com/browse/purpose.

(2) Collins English Dictionary, 10th ed., Dictionary.com, accessed 08/01/2010,
http://dictionary.reference.com/browse/reason.

(3) Norman Herr P.h.D. "A.C. Neilson Ratings," The Sourcebook for Teaching Science, accessed 08/01/2010,
http://www.csun.edu/science/health/docs/tv&health.html.

Chapter 4

(1) Mattathias Schwartz, "Dome Sweet Dome" *Bloomberg Businessweek* August 2-8 2010, 64-67

Chapter 5

(1) Dictionary.com, accessed 08/20/2010,
http://dictionary.reference.com/browse/integrity.

(2) Online Etymology Dictionary, accessed 10/08/2010,
http://www.etymonline.com/index.php?term=integrity.

(3) Marine Corp Leadership Traits, Center for Strategic Leadership Studies, accessed 10/08/2010,
http://www.au.af.mil/au/awc/awcgate/usmc/leadership_traits.htm.

Chapter 7

    (1) Influence Definition wordnetweb.princeton.edu
http://wordnetweb.princeton.edu/perl/webwn?s=Influence&sub
=Search+WordNet&o2=&o0=1&o7=&o5=&o1=1&o6=&o4=
&o3=&h= Accessed 09/10/2010

Chapter 8

    (1) Letter dated January 1, 1863 from Abraham Lincoln to Major
General Hooker regarding command of the Army of the Potomac. AbrahamLincolnonline.org, accessed 7/10/2010,
http://showcase.netins.net/web/creative/lincoln/speeches/hooke
r.htm

Chapter 10

    (1) Aristotle, "Rhetoric,"
    (2) Kurt and Brenda Warner, *First Things First* (Tyndale House
Publishers, 2009).
    (3) John C. Maxwell and Les Parrott, *Twenty-Five Ways to Win
with People* (Nashville, TN: Thomas Nelson, Inc. 2005).
    (4) Survey of time wasted by employees, salary.com, accessed
7/10/2010,
http://www.salary.com/Articles/ArticleDetail.asp?part=par108
3.

Chapter11

    (1) Tamara Lowe, *Get Motivated* (New York, NY: Double-
day/Random House, Inc., 2009).
    (2) Susan G. Komen for the Cure, ww5.komen.org, accessed
12/23/10, http://ww5.komen.org/AboutUs/AboutUs.html.

Chapter 12

(1) Don Soderquist, *The Wal-Mart Way* (Nashville, TN: Thomas Nelson, Inc., 2005).

(2) Walmart ranks as #1 retailer in the World CNNMoney.com http://money.cnn.com/magazines/fortune/global500/2010/snapshots/2255.html 09/26/2010 Accessed

(3) Walmart Net sales 405 billion, Walmart.com, http://walmartstores.com/AboutUs/ 09/26/2010 Accessed

Chapter 15

(1) Napoleon Hill, *Think and Grow Rich* (Chicago, Il: Combined Registry Company, 1962).

(2) John Maxwell, *Mentoring 101*(Nashville, TN: Thomas Nelson Inc., 2008).

Chapter 16

(1) Dan Green, *More Than a Hobby* (Nashville, TN: Thomas Nelson, Inc., 2005).

(2) Timothy J. Koegel, *The Exceptional Presenter* (Austin, TX: Greenleaf Book Group, 2007).

About the Author

Justin lives in middle Tennessee with his wife and three children. He is recognized as an expert in sales, leadership and personal development. He is the author of *Power Words for the Sales Professional*, and the popular *103 Proven Sales Tips* that has been studied by sales professionals worldwide.

Justin's diverse professional career in politics, law enforcement and business allows him to bring fresh perspectives to the discussion. His unique ability to connect with an audience has made him a sought after speaker. His workshops and seminars on Sales, Leadership and Personal Development are inspiring a new generation to reach past their potential.

Connect with Justin at,

www.JustinHammonds.com

"Don't be afraid to give up the good to go for the great."

-John D. Rockefeller

"Good enough never is."

-Debbi Fields

www.ingramcontent.com/pod-product-compliance
Lightning Source LLC
Chambersburg PA
CBHW060016210326
41520CB00009B/909